INDIGENOUS PEOPLES OF NORTH AMERICA

INDIGENOUS PEOPLES OF NORTH AMERICA

A CONCISE ANTHROPOLOGICAL OVERVIEW

ROBERT J. MUCKLE

UNIVERSITY OF TORONTO PRESS

Library and Archives Canada Cataloguing in Publication

Muckle, Robert James
    Indigenous peoples of North America : a concise anthropological overview / Robert J. Muckle.

Includes bibliographical references and index.
Also issued in electronic format.
ISBN 978-1-4426-0356-1

    1. Indians of North America. 1. Title.

E77.M89 2012   970.004 97   C2011-908502-X

We welcome comments and suggestions regarding any aspect of our publications—please feel free
to contact us at news@utphighereducation.com or visit our Internet site at www.utppublishing.com.

North America
5201 Dufferin Street
North York, Ontario, Canada, M3H 5T8

2250 Military Road
Tonawanda, New York, USA, 14150

ORDERS PHONE: 1–800–565–9523
ORDERS FAX: 1–800–221–9985
ORDERS E-MAIL: utpbooks@utpress.utoronto.ca

UK, Ireland, and continental Europe
NBN International
Estover Road, Plymouth, PL6 7PY, UK
ORDERS PHONE: 44 (0) 1752 202301
ORDERS FAX: 44 (0) 1752 202333
ORDERS E-MAIL: enquiries@nbninternational.com

Every effort has been made to contact copyright holders; in the event of an error or omission,
please notify the publisher.

The University of Toronto Press acknowledges the financial support for its publishing activities of
the Government of Canada through the Canada Book Fund.

Designed by Daiva Villa, Chris Rowat Design

CONTENTS

ILLUSTRATIONS

TABLES

BOXES

PREFACE

This book is for those who would like a fundamental knowledge of the Indigenous peoples of North America, also known as Natives, Native Americans, Indians, First Nations, First Peoples, Aboriginals, and other labels. Through the lens of anthropology, this book offers clarity in the comprehensive, often complex, and sometimes confusing area of Indigenous, Native, or Indian studies.

This book was conceived primarily as a core textbook for undergraduate anthropology courses at the college and university levels. In this sense, the book is deliberately concise. It provides a basic foundation from which instructors can build, depending on their own interests, expertise, and objectives. It is envisioned that most instructors will supplement the book with other resources.

Secondly, this book was conceived as a supplemental textbook for other courses in the social sciences and humanities. This includes general or introductory courses in anthropology or related disciplines where the book may be used to expand, clarify, or provide examples or alternate frameworks for core course material. The book may also be used to provide context or background information in non-anthropology courses that focus on Indigenous peoples; and as a basic reference or handbook for those with an interest in the Indigenous peoples of North America, be they academic, professional, or lay audiences.

This book introduces and provides basic information on the broad themes of study of the Indigenous peoples of the North American continent, including the vast archaeological record, traditional lifeways, the impacts of colonialization, and contemporary issues. It provides a context from which instructors or students can begin further study and discussion; offers multiple opportunities to compare relevant histories and issues in the United States and Canada; and considers the Indigenous peoples of the continent, and the anthropology of these many groups, in a global perspective.

This book has an explicit anthropological perspective. In practical terms, this means that it is structured around major themes of traditional anthropological interest such as prehistory, traditional lifeways, and culture change, as well as areas of current anthropological interest such as assertions of rights and identity, intellectual property rights, and the appropriation of culture. Using an anthropological perspective also means that the book is framed around evolutionary, comparative, and holistic approaches. Anthropological terminology and concepts are utilized throughout.

Anthropologists and others with an interest in the Indigenous peoples often use a particular vocabulary. Readers may come across words they have never seen before or words being used in unfamiliar ways. In order to alleviate confusion, these words are identified in bold type the first time they appear in the text, and described more fully in the Glossary.

The book provides a relatively normative anthropological approach to the study of the Indigenous peoples and cultures of North America, albeit in a very concise way. Not all anthropologists would choose to cover the topic in the way it is presented in this book, but there is nothing radical in it. Where there is controversy or debate, the book identifies the controversies and generally takes the middle ground. It has been written by a non-Indigenous, middle-aged male of primarily European descent with a passion for education, anthropology, and doing what he can to address an awful lot of misinformation and confusion about the Indigenous peoples of North America. I have been informed by many years of study and considerable interaction with Indigenous peoples, both in consulting work and in educational institutions, and many of these people have become friends. I make no claim, however, of offering an Indigenous insider's view of Indigenous life and experiences. My view is that of an anthropologist.

A NOTE ON CLASSIFICATION, TERMINOLOGY, AND SPELLING

Not everyone will agree with the terminology, classifications, and spellings used in this book. There is little consensus on how academics, governments, the general public, and Indigenous peoples themselves classify, describe, and spell the names of people, places, and events as they relate to the Indigenous peoples of North America. The classifications, terminology, and spellings used in this book tend to reflect recent trends, but are subject to debate and change.

ACKNOWLEDGEMENTS

I owe thanks to quite a few people. I am appreciative of all I have learned from the many Indigenous peoples of North America I have worked with over the past few decades. This includes many members of the many different Indigenous nations who welcomed me into their communities, allowing me to pursue my passion in anthropology and providing me insight into their cultures and lives. I was able to establish myself as a professional in the areas of anthropology and Indigenous Studies early in my career through the support of Indigenous leaders, including several former chiefs of the Pacific Northwest Salishan Nations, especially those of the Secwepemc (Shuswap), including Edna Louis (Simpcw/North Thompson), Nathan Matthew (Simpcw/North Thompson), Ron Ignace (Skeetchstn), and Gerald (Gerry) Etienne (Stuctwewsemc/Bonaparte). One day while working with Gerry I asked him why he thought it was that I was able to find so much work with Indigenous groups while others with similar academic credentials and experience weren't. Without hesitation, he explained that it was easy. First, he said, it was because I actually listened to them and didn't just pretend. Second, he said that it was known I could be trusted, and that knowledge spreads quickly through the "Indian grapevine." For that, I am eternally grateful. I also owe Gerry gratitude for showing me the fine art of hunting rattlesnakes, often acting as a decoy.

I have been fortunate in my college and university career to have had dozens of opportunities to teach anthropology to many Native Americans, both in large urban centers and in their home communities. I feel fortunate that the leaders of many of the Indigenous groups close to where I have lived and worked have valued anthropology and encouraged their members to take anthropology courses, especially those of the Lil'wat, Nlaka'pamux, Nicola Valley, Nuxalk, Okanagan, Sechelt, Secwepemc, Snuneymuxw, Squamish, and Tseil Waututh nations. I place a high value on the support I have received from Indigenous students in the way I teach them and others about Indigenous peoples of North America. I have learned much from many of these students, both informally (outside the classroom and especially in their home communities) and formally (in the classroom when they choose to share information, cultural performances, perspectives, and experiences). Many have provided insight into their lives and cultures, as well as assisting me to achieve and maintain credibility in the eyes of others. In this regard I am particularly grateful to Syexwaliya/Ann Whonnock (Squamish Nation), Yumks/Rudy Reimer (Squamish Nation) and Jamie Thomas (Snuneymuxw).

I am grateful for the ability to regularly converse with other anthropologists who are as passionate about the anthropological study of Indigenous peoples of North America as I am. Foremost in this regard is a fellow anthropologist specializing in Indigenous peoples of North America, Thomas (Tad) McIlwraith. Tad has extensive experience working with Indigenous peoples and with teaching undergraduate courses about Indigenous peoples. I place a high value on his support of my writing this book the way I have, as well as his acting as a sounding board for my ideas. In addition to providing support, Tad also provided a very detailed review of my original manuscript with many useful suggestions. I am also thankful for the positive support of the anonymous reviewers of the original book proposal who supported my belief that there was a place for a book like this, and the anonymous reviewers of the manuscript who offered positive and constructive comments.

I am grateful for the positive work environment in the Department of Anthropology at Capilano University and the support of all my colleagues while writing this book: Gillian Crowther, Maureen Bracewell, and Cassandra Bill. I appreciate their acting as sounding boards for my thoughts and for taking on more than their fair share of departmental tasks so that I could write. Gillian was also very helpful in creating the maps for this book. My friend, colleague in anthropology, and photographer extraordinaire Barry Kass was very helpful in the process of selecting photos.

Further appreciation is due the staff at the University of Toronto Press, particularly executive editor Anne Brackenbury, who has guided me through this book from the initial idea to publication. I am also grateful for the editing undertaken by Nina Hoeschele of The Editing Company who has made me appear to be a better writer than I really am.

ONE

SITUATING THE INDIGENOUS PEOPLES OF NORTH AMERICA

INTRODUCTION

There are close to 6 million people living in North America who identify as Indigenous, or one of the other popular labels such as Aboriginal, Indian, or Native American. They comprise about 2 per cent of the population and live in every state, province, and territory of the continent, some in rural areas and others in cities. They are doctors, lawyers, and Indian chiefs. They are also teachers, police, firefighters, politicians, judges, musicians, actors, childcare workers, nurses, truck drivers, writers, and more. Some who may appear to be Indian aren't; and many who do not appear to be Indian are. The extreme diversity of Indigenous cultures is reflected in the fact that more than 1,000 distinct tribal entities or nations continue to exist today. This book, and especially this chapter, seek to offer some clarity in the often confusing terminology and sense of Indigenous identity, lands, and populations.

The objective of this chapter is to lay the groundwork for studying the **Indigenous** peoples of **North America**. This includes clarifying what is meant by "North America"; outlining the uses and meanings of various labels by which the Indigenous peoples of North America are known; providing an overview of the contemporary demography and organizational structures of the Indigenous peoples of North America; and considering the Indigenous peoples of North America from a global perspective.

NORTH AMERICA DEFINED

The way one conceptualizes North America is often based on perspective and context. There are multiple ways of viewing the land, based on a variety of physical and cultural characteristics.

For those with backgrounds or primary interests in geography, history, politics, or business, it often makes sense to view North America as one of two continents or as one of three regions, based on geography or contemporary national boundaries. For some, the entire landmass in the western hemisphere—stretching from the Arctic in the north to Cape Horn in the south—is simply divided into the two continents of North America and South America, separated by the Panama Canal. Others recognize three main geographical regions known as North, Central, and South America; or North, Middle, and South America. Some people consider Mexico to be part of North America while others include Mexico as part of Central or Middle America. Depending on the context, the islands of the Caribbean may be considered as part of North America, Central America, Middle America, or Latin America.

While some anthropologists include all of Mexico and the islands of the Caribbean as part of North America, most do not. Anthropologists typically view the western hemisphere as being divided into the three broad cultural regions of North America, **Mesoamerica**, and South America. The distinctions are based on very broad similarities in Indigenous histories and cultures. In this view, the northern part of Mexico is usually considered to be part of North America while the central and southern parts are considered to be part of Mesoamerica.

The arbitrary line between North America and Mesoamerica excludes the peoples of some of the well-known Indigenous civilizations, such as the Maya and the Aztec, from North America, even though their influence is evident in some North American groups—especially in the south-west United States.

Although some anthropologists frame their studies of the Indigenous peoples of North America to include all of Mexico and sometimes other Central American countries as well, it is most common for anthropologists specializing in the Indigenous peoples of North America to view "North America" from a cultural rather than geographical perspective. Consequently, their definition generally includes all of Canada, the continental United States (including Alaska), Greenland, and northern Mexico.

Hawaii and Greenland are rarely explicitly considered in anthropological overviews or generalizations about North America. To start with, Hawaii is not usually considered to be part of the physical region of North America. Further, since the Indigenous peoples of Hawaii have a closer affinity to cultures of Polynesia than they do to those on continental North America, Hawaii is not usually considered to be part of North America by anthropologists interested in the prehistory, traditional lifeways, and impacts of European colonialism. An exception, of course, is when anthropologists

FIGURE 1.1
North America, as Conceptualized by Most Anthropologists

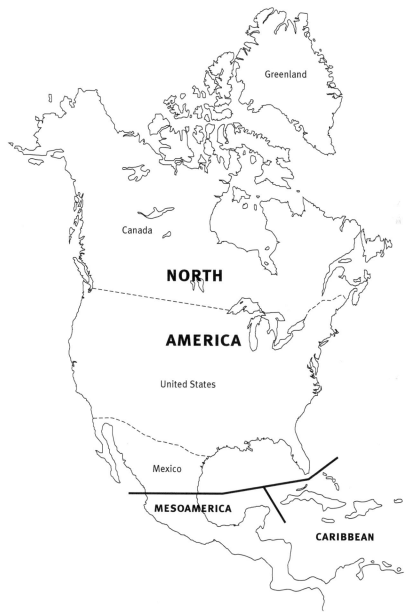

choose to focus on Indigenous peoples based on the political boundaries of the United States.

By contrast, Greenland is usually considered to be part of North America by geographers and anthropologists. Not only is the landmass generally considered as part of the physical region known as North America, but Greenland's Indigenous people also have a common origin and continue to share cultural similarities with the Indigenous peoples of the Canadian Arctic.

In this book, North America is taken to mean all of Canada, the continental United States (including Alaska), Greenland, and the northern part of Mexico. The islands of the Caribbean are not considered to be part of North America in this book. In other words, the book focuses on the Indigenous cultures north of Mesoamerica. Because of the relatively low population numbers and broad cultural similarities to those living in the American south-west, the Indigenous peoples of north Mexico receive little distinct attention in this book. Similarly, scant attention is focused on the Indigenous peoples of Greenland due to their small population and similarities to the Canadian Inuit.

This book's concept of North America (i.e., the area north of Mesoamerica, of which the boundary between North America and Mesoamerica runs in an east-west direction through northern Mexico) is consistent with many other overviews of Indigenous peoples and cultures of North America—including the multi-volume *Handbook of North American Indians*, published by the Smithsonian Institution, which is considered by many to be a standard source for the study of the Indigenous peoples of North America.

It is worth noting that some Indigenous people reject the very label of "North America" based on the notion that the label itself is a product of European imperialism. (It was named after an Italian explorer—Amerigo Vespucci—by a German cartographer.) In its place, some Indigenous people and groups use alternate names, such as **Turtle Island** (based on origin stories in the mythology of some groups). Conceptions of land and space, as well as origin myths, vary widely between Indigenous people and groups, however; and while Turtle Island is widely recognized as an Indigenous label for North America, not all Indigenous people use it.

INDIGENOUS, INDIAN, NATIVE AMERICAN, FIRST NATION, ABORIGINAL, AND OTHER LABELS

There is no shortage of labels to describe the Indigenous peoples of North America. Use of various labels is often a reflection of context or interest. In this book, Indigenous is used as a collective term to describe those who trace their ancestry to the inhabitants of North America before the

FIGURE 1.2

Hierarchy of Labels for the Indigenous Peoples of the United States and Canada

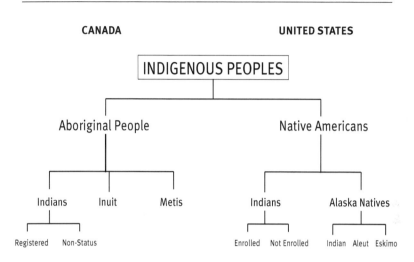

arrival of Europeans in the early 1500s. Figure 1.2 clarifies the distinctions between some of the most widely used terms.

Indigenous has become increasingly popular in its usage to describe the descendants of a land's original inhabitants, both globally and within North America. Indigenous is widely considered to include those who claim ancestry from a self-governing society that inhabited a region before the invasion, conquest, settlement, or other form of occupation by people of different cultures who then became dominant.

The United Nations Permanent Forum on Indigenous Issues suggests that self-identification is a fundamental criterion of being recognized as an Indigenous person. Other criteria include having historical continuity with pre-colonial or pre-settler societies; having a strong link to territory and resources; having a distinct culture; forming a non-dominant group within society; and having a resolve to maintain one's distinct characteristics. In most instances, Indigenous peoples are also characterized by being both economically and socially marginalized within the dominant societies in which they exist.

On a global scale, "Indigenous" has in many instances replaced terms such as **Indians**, Natives, and **Aboriginals**, and is now widely used in North America and elsewhere around the world. It is now common for groups to self-identify as Indigenous, which at least for some serves as a political strategy and provides them with a voice on the world stage, such as the United Nations. Indigenous groups from North America, for example, worked with Indigenous peoples elsewhere in the formulation of the United Nations Declaration on the Rights of Indigenous Peoples, adopted by the General Assembly in 2007 (see Appendix 1).

Organizations and people recognize and apply "indigenism" in different ways. The United Nations, for example, recognizes indigeneity around the globe, making no distinction pertaining to place. Others recognize distinct kinds of indigenism—for example, New World Indigenism, which applies to the Indigenous peoples and cultures of the Americas, Australia, and New Zealand that came under the domination of Europeans and European nations over the past several hundred years. Some recognize the experience of New World Indigenism as being distinct from the oppression suffered by some less powerful ethnic groups under more powerful ones, such as occurs frequently in Africa and Asia.

In this book, Indigenous is used to refer to all the people who are accepted as members of federally recognized Indigenous groups (e.g., bands or First Nations in Canada; tribes or tribal entity in the US) as well as people who claim ancestry to the occupants of the land before the arrival of Europeans, but who may not meet the criteria for membership established by governments or Indigenous groups.

The reason for using the Indigenous label in this book is threefold. First, it simplifies things by unifying several common and legal labels, hundreds of distinct groups, and millions of individuals claiming ancestry to those who occupied North America before the arrival of Europeans. Second, the use of the term "Indigenous" is consistent with the increasing popularity of the term in both mainstream and academic cultures within North America (e.g., book and journal titles, indigenous studies programs). Third, since contextualizing the Indigenous peoples of North America within a global context of indigeneity is a theme that runs through the text, it seems appropriate to use the terminology that is most common within the global context.

It should be recognized that most labels that have been, and continue to be, applied to the Indigenous peoples of North America have been coined by non-Indigenous people for use as collective terms. They do not necessarily reflect how Indigenous peoples identified themselves before these labels began to appear, or how they identify themselves today.

It is common for Indigenous people to affiliate most closely with a specific group, such as Cherokee, Cree, Mohawk, Navajo, or one of the hundreds of other distinctive Indigenous ethnic groups. In many cases, the Indigenous peoples reject the labels imposed upon them by Europeans and those of European descent, preferring instead to refer to themselves by

TABLE 1.1
Common Indigenous Labels in the United States and Canada

Indigenous
Commonly used around the world, and increasingly being used in North America, as a collective term to describe people formerly known as Natives, Aboriginals, and Indians.

Aboriginal
Rarely used in the United States, but commonly used in Canada as a collective term for Indian, Inuit, and Metis.

Eskimo
Commonly used in the United States to refer to the Indigenous peoples of Arctic Alaska.

First Nation
Commonly used in Canada; rare in the United States.

Indian
A legal and common term used in both the United States and Canada. Remains in wide use in the United States, but less often in Canada.

Inuit
The common term used in Canada to describe the Indigenous peoples of Arctic Canada, replacing "Eskimo."

Native American
A term used widely in the United States to include both Indians and Alaska Natives; rarely used in Canada.

their own names, in their own languages—such as "Lakota" or "Dakota" in place of Sioux; and "Dine" in place of Navajo. Depending on context, they may also affiliate themselves with smaller groups, perhaps reflective of a small band or settlement within a larger ethnic group. In other contexts, they may choose to identify with larger regional, national, continental, or global entities.

The term Indigenous replaces, or subsumes within it, many different labels. Some of these are listed and described in Table 1.1.

It is commonly held that the label "Indian" was imposed upon the Indigenous peoples of all of the Americas following the belief that Christopher Columbus had reached India (rather than what we now know as the Americas) in 1492. Some have commented that this belief itself may be based on an error in translation, and that Columbus knew he had not arrived in India. It has been suggested, for example, that "Indian" may have been based on Columbus's use of the phrase "*una gente in Dios,*" meaning "people of God."

Although there have been many criticisms of the use of the term "Indian," it remains in wide use by governments and individuals in the United States and Canada, where it is both a legal term and a common descriptor of Indigenous peoples of North America.

"Natives" or "Native Peoples" is common terminology in both Canada and the United States. It has legal status for some Indigenous groups in Alaska (i.e., "**Alaska Natives**"), and is used by some associations (e.g., United Native Nations), but it is mostly a common descriptor with no legal status.

Some attempts have been made to distinguish Indians of North America from elsewhere, such as those currently living in or descended from those living in India, or the Indigenous populations of South America (sometimes known as South American Indians). These efforts have resulted in such labels as "American Indian," "North American Indian," and "Ameri-Indian."

"Aboriginal" is sometimes considered synonymous with Indian or Native. The term is not common in the United States but is frequently used in Canada; for example, "Aboriginal" is used in the Canadian Constitution (1982) to include Indian, **Inuit**, and **Metis**.

First Nations and **First Peoples** are common descriptors of those formerly or otherwise known as Indians—but not Metis or Inuit—in Canada. Many Indigenous peoples in Canada prefer to use "First Nations" to describe both individuals and groups. This is for multiple reasons, including that its origin and continued use has primarily been an initiative of the people themselves, rather than being a label applied by governments, anthropologists, and others of mainstream, non-Indigenous societies; it alleviates negative connotations often associated with other descriptors; it emphasizes the ancestors of the peoples who occupied the lands first (i.e., before Europeans); the word "nation" reflects sovereignty; and the plural recognizes the distinctiveness of groups. However, although the descriptors "First Nations" and "First Peoples" have readily been adopted by many in Canadian society, "Indian" and "Native" have not been totally replaced; usage of those terms continues among both Indigenous and non-Indigenous individuals and groups.

Most Indigenous groups in the far North have been called **Eskimo**, and this term remains in use for some groups in Alaska. In Canada, Eskimo has largely been replaced by the term Inuit. The Indigenous peoples of Greenland are known by various terms, including Inuit, Polar Eskimo, Greenland Eskimo, and Kalaaliit.

The situation in Mexico is a bit different. Compared to the United States and Canada, there is a much larger percentage of people with Indigenous ancestry in Mexico, and it has been reported that about 20 per cent of the population is fully Indigenous; about 75 per cent have mixed Indigenous and non-Indigenous ancestry; and only about 5 per cent have no North American Indigenous ancestry. Those of mixed ancestry are commonly referred to as **mestizo**, and those who speak an Indigenous language are often called **Indios** or Indigenas.

OVERVIEW OF THE INDIGENOUS PEOPLES OF NORTH AMERICA TODAY

Identity

It is common for Indigenous people in North America to identify with being citizens of both the country in which they reside (e.g., the United States, Canada, Greenland, or northern Mexico) as well as an Indigenous nation. There are some Indigenous people that reject the identity of being a citizen of the United States or Canada; and there are other Indigenous people that choose to reject their rights to citizenship in an Indigenous nation. Most, however, are comfortable with living in both worlds.

Many Indigenous people have their feet in multiple worlds, including that of their specific Indigenous nation; the larger national, continental, or global Indigenous movements; and their country of citizenship, with its own distinctive culture (e.g., modern American culture). Figure 1.3 illustrates a father and daughter waiting for the dancing to begin at a **powwow** in Missoula, Montana. The very existence of a powwow is part of the contemporary North American Indigenous world, with roots extending back into prehistory, especially in the Plains area. The father and daughter in the photograph are maintaining their Indigenous culture through their clothing and participation, but there is room for modernity as well; the powwow is being held in a modern structure and the father is using a cell phone. Indigenous peoples and anthropologists recognize that cultures are in a continual state of change; elements of tradition and modernity coexist. It is a mistake to think that cultures are static—or that Indigenous people are forced to choose between one culture and another. In reality, both cultures and peoples are constantly in flux.

Distinct categories of Indigenous peoples are recognized in both the United States and Canada. In the United States, the Indigenous peoples are often collectively referred to as **Native Americans**. Those of the "lower 48" are commonly referred to as Indians, while those in Alaska are usually called Alaska Natives; this is a collective term used for a wide range of groups in Alaska, including those labeled as Indian, Eskimo, or Aleut.

In Canada, three distinct kinds of Indigenous peoples are recognized. Aboriginal is the collective term, with major subgroups of Indian, Inuit, and Metis. Each term is entrenched in the Canadian Constitution, which was patriated in 1982. Section 35 of the Constitution states, in part:

(1) The existing aboriginal and treaty rights of the aboriginal peoples of Canada are hereby recognized and affirmed.

(2) In this Act, "aboriginal peoples of Canada" includes Indian, Inuit, and Metis peoples of Canada.

FIGURE 1.3 Waiting for the Dancing to Begin at a Powwow. A father and daughter, of the Crow Nation, at a powwow in Missoula, Montana. (Photo © Sings in the Timber Photography / Adam Sings in the Timber. Reprinted by permission.)

Although "Indian" is used widely by the United States government, there is no single definition of the term used by all government agencies. One survey revealed that there are more than 30 different definitions of "Indian" in federal legislation. The federal Bureau of Indian Affairs acknowledges that there is no single federal or tribal standard for considering someone an Indian or Alaska Native, but indicates that as a general rule, a person claiming status as an American Indian or Alaska Native should have some blood ties to a federally recognized tribe and be enrolled as a member of that tribe. The various government agencies that have programs for Indians and Alaska Natives use differing criteria to determine who is eligible for their programs. Thus, while an individual may be a member of a recognized tribe, he or she may not necessarily be eligible for federal programs for Indians.

In the United States, Indians that are recognized by the federal government and are members of a federally recognized tribal entity are considered **enrolled.** Being recognized as a member of a tribal entity is often the first step towards being recognized by the federal government and obtaining the benefits of that recognition. This results in a broad division between those claiming to be Indian—those who are enrolled, and subsequently entitled to the benefits of enrollment—and those who are not enrolled and therefore not entitled to benefits. Those in this second group are sometimes called the **Outalucks** or **Wannabees**.

There are also two broad divisions within the Indian community in Canada: **registered Indians** and **non-status Indians**. Registered Indians are also known as **status Indians**. If a person is "Registered," it means that their name appears on a register maintained by the federal government. Unlike the United States, blood ties or affiliation with a specific Indigenous group have never been required for government recognition as an Indian in Canada. Besides ancestry, eligibility for registered status has included such things as marriage, education, and occupation. A non-Indian woman, for example, could obtain status by marrying a status Indian, and in the past registered Indians could lose their status if they obtained a university education or joined the military.

In both the United States and Canada, certificates are issued to individuals to prove their Indian status. In the United States, the Bureau of Indian Affairs issues a "Certificate of Degree of Indian Blood," commonly referred to as a **CDIB**, and which specifies the degree of Indian blood the person has, known as **blood quantum**. In Canada, the federal agency responsible for Indigenous peoples, Aboriginal Affairs and Northern Development Canada, issues a **status card** to registered Indians.

Identity as an Indian or as a member of another recognized Indigenous group is important for those in both the United States and Canada, and for several reasons. For many, the recognition is important for social, political, ideological, and personal reasons. Recognition also provides access to social, health, and educational programs, and may bring economic benefits through treaties, other agreements, and Indigenous-run business ventures.

In both the United States and Canada, obtaining membership in a particular Indigenous group is not always easy. It can be complex and confusing (see Box 1.1, "Indian Identity"). The federal government in each country has agreed to let the individual Indigenous groups create their own criteria for membership. Most groups require some level of blood quantum to become a member, although the percentage of blood required

---

BOX 1.1
Indian Identity

Indian identity is often complex and confusing. Federal governments have their own criteria and many of the more than 1,000 federally recognized Indigenous groups have separate criteria.

In *Real Indians: Identity and the Survival of Native America*, Eva Marie Garroutte (2003) discusses four different ways of defining Indianness: legal, biological, cultural, and personal. Garroutte also outlines the process of being a legal Indian, which is primarily based on blood quantum, although that in itself does not make becoming a legal Indian simple. "Indian" is defined in almost three dozen different ways in United States federal legislation, and there is no standard for the blood quantum that allows recognition as a tribal member among the various groups. Wide-ranging criteria create situations where people with no biological ties to Indigenous peoples past or present have legal Indian identities while others with clear Indigenous ancestry do not. Since many benefits may come with legal Indian identity, some describe this latter group as belonging to the category of the "Outalucks." Among those with legal status, there is often factionalism between those with half- or full-blood status and those with a lesser percentage, which can lead to discrimination within Indigenous groups. Cultural identity often comes into play when trying to satisfy requirements imposed on groups seeking federal recognition or in other cases where the establishment of Indian identity is required, such as in placing children in foster homes or legal cases involving Aboriginal rights.

In *Blood Politics: Race, Culture, and Identity in the Cherokee Nation of Oklahoma*, Circe Sturm (2002) focuses specifically on the construction of Cherokee identity. Cherokee tribal law requires new members to be lineal descendants of an enrolled member (i.e., listed on the Dawes Roll, created by government in the 1800s), but there is no minimum blood quantum. As a result, it is possible to be an enrolled member of the Cherokee Nation with less than one two-thousandth Cherokee blood. This means that an enrolled Cherokee could be as many as ten generations removed from a full-blood Cherokee who lived during the 1700s.

---

varies widely. It is common for some groups to require anywhere between one-quarter and one-32nd blood quantum. Some groups, however, require as much as one-half, and at the other extreme, some groups require only a lineal blood tie to a recognized member. This is the case with the Cherokee, for example, whose members may be as many as ten generations removed from anyone with Cherokee blood.

In some cases, groups may require a person's blood quantum to be specific to the group they seek membership in. This results in situations where people of mixed ancestry may exceed the minimum requirements of blood quantum overall, except that they do not have the minimum blood quantum for any specific group, and so they are not eligible for membership in those groups. Thus some people whose blood is a quarter or more Indian may have no official Indian identity, while others who are ten or more generations removed may be registered.

Some groups require blood quantum be determined through either the paternal or maternal line; some specify that it must be through the maternal line; and others specify that it must be through the paternal line. Thus the children of a mother from a tribe that determines descent only through the father's line and a father from a tribe that determines descent only through the mother's line may have 100 per cent Indian blood, and yet fail to meet the membership requirements of both the mother's and the father's tribes.

Basic Organization

The basic unit of economic and political organization of most recognized Indigenous people in Canada today is the band or First Nation. In the United States, the basic economic and political units are called tribes in the "lower 48" states, and Alaska Native villages or village groups in Alaska.

"Band" and "tribe" each have multiple meanings. In anthropology, the terms are often used to describe traditional forms of political organization, based on a variety of criteria including group size, interaction spheres, and forms of leadership (described more fully in Chapter 4). However, this is not the most common meaning of the words when describing contemporary Indigenous peoples and groups in North America, and the terms band and tribe are used to describe these organizations in different ways. In contemporary times, bands and tribes are merely organizational structures created largely for the purpose of administration. In some cases, multiple self-governing groups were arbitrarily formed into a single band or tribe, while in other cases single self-governing groups were divided into multiple bands or tribes. Prior to the arrival of Europeans, most Indigenous groups were far more complex than is implied by the terms band or tribe.

The Canadian government defines "band" as "a body of Indians...for whose use and benefit in common, lands, the legal title to which is vested in Her Majesty, have been set apart" (Indian Act, 1989).

The United States Bureau of Indian Affairs describes a "federally recognized tribe" as

an American Indian or Alaska Native tribal entity that is recognized as having a government to government relationship with the United States, with the responsibilities, powers, limitations, and obligations attributed to that designation, and is eligible for funding and services from the Bureau of Indian Affairs. Furthermore, federally recognized tribes are recognized as possessing certain inherent rights of self-government (i.e. tribal sovereignty) and are entitled to receive certain federal benefits, services, and protection because of the special relationship with the United States.

TABLE 1.2

Basic Data on Population, Bands and Tribes, and Indian Lands

United States
Approximate number of enrolled members: 2 million
Approximate total number of those claiming Indigenous ancestry: 4.5 million
Total claiming Indigenous ancestry as percentage of total US population: 1.5 per cent
Total number of federally recognized tribal entities (Tribes and Alaska Native Villages): 564
Total number of reservations: approximately 300
Total number of acres of reservations and lands controlled by Alaska Natives:
    approximately 150 million acres

Canada
Approximate number of registered Indians: 630,000
Approximate number of those claiming Indigenous ancestry: 1.2 million
Total claiming Indigenous ancestry as a total of Canadian population: 4 per cent
Total number of federally recognized bands or First Nations: 615
Total number of reserves: approximately 2,300
Total number of acres of reserves: approximately 6.8 million

North American Totals
Approximate number of federally recognized Indigenous people: 2.6 million
Approximate total number claiming Indigenous ancestry: 5.7 million
Total claiming Indigenous ancestry as a percentage of the North American population:
    2 per cent
Total number of federally recognized Indigenous groups: 1,145

In both countries, alternate names are sometimes used. Although band or Indian band remains a legal term in Canada, "First Nation" or "Nation" is now commonly used by governments, Indigenous peoples, anthropologists, other academics, and the public. In the United States, "tribe" is used most commonly. Alternatives to those terms in both countries include council, village, association, community, and corporation. Some Indigenous people and groups reject all of these terms, choosing instead to use words from their own languages.

Although the band or tribe is a basic unit of organization for many purposes, including maintaining relations with governments, many Indigenous people identify first with a distinct ethnic group, such as Apache, Cherokee, Hopi, Mohawk, Navajo, or one of the hundreds of other existing groups. In some cases the ethnic group equates with a federally recognized band or tribe, but in many cases it does not (i.e., many traditional ethnic groups have subsequently been reorganized into separate bands or tribes; and some historically distinct ethnic groups were combined to form a distinct band or tribe).

Federally recognized groups in both Canada and the United States usually have a structural organization similar to various non-Indigenous, democratic governments. This includes elected representatives, often known in Indigenous communities as **chief** and council. "Chief" is common for the leader, but alternatives include chair (or chairman, chairwoman, or chairperson), president, governor, mayor, spokesperson, or representative. Basic data about population, numbers of bands and tribes, and land are listed in Table 1.2.

There are several hundred federally recognized Indigenous groups in each of Canada and the United States, with a total population of approximately 3 million people. Adding those people who claim Indigenous identities, but are not recognized as such by the federal governments, doubles the total number to approximately 6 million.

There are 615 Indian Bands or First Nations recognized by the Canadian government. Approximately 630,000 people identify as "Registered Indian" (i.e., recognized by the Canadian government and/or an individual band or nation). However, almost 1.2 million people claim Aboriginal identity (i.e., affiliating with Indian, Inuit, or Metis), accounting for about 4 per cent of the Canadian population.

In the United States there are 564 recognized tribal entities (i.e., Indian tribes and Alaska Native villages), with approximately 2 million enrolled members. However, according to census data and other population estimates, more than double that number identify as having American Indian or Alaska Native ancestry (4.5 million), accounting for about 1.5 per cent of the American population.

Reserves, Reservations, and Other Indian Lands

Indian lands is a term used to describe lands set aside by the governments of Canada and the United States for Indigenous peoples. In Canada these lands are usually called **reserves**, while in the United States they are usually called **reservations**. Besides the lands that are typically understood as reservations, in the United States the category of "Indian reservation" also includes pueblos, rancherias, missions, villages, colonies, and communities.

There is little consistency in the number, size, and location of Indian lands for Indigenous groups. Many Indigenous groups have multiple reserves or reservations, and some have none. In Canada there are more than 2,300 reserves totaling a land area of 6.8 million acres, but most are relatively small and unoccupied. Many are forested. In the US there are more than 300 land areas administered by the federal government as federal Indian reservations, totaling 56.2 million acres. The smallest is a 1.3 acre piece of land in California, while the largest is the 16 million acre Navajo reservation comprising portions of Arizona, New Mexico, and Utah. Both in Canada and the US, the Indian lands are usually, but not always, within a group's traditional territory or homeland.

FIGURE 1.4 Taos Pueblo, New Mexico. This site has been consistently occupied for at least 1,000 years, and has been designated a World Heritage Site by the United Nations. Pueblos are one kind of Indian lands reserved for use by Indigenous peoples. (Photo © Barry D. Kass@ ImagesofAnthropology.com. Reprinted by permission.)

FIGURE 1.5 Iqaluit, Nunavut. Meaning "place of many fishes" in the Inuktitut language of the Inuit, Iqaluit is the capital of Nunavut, a territory largely governed by Inuit, and which officially came into being in 1999. Iqaluit has a population of about 7,000, making it the largest community in Nunavut, which itself is about the size of Western Europe. (Photo © Leslie Coates / Arcticnet. Reprinted by permission.)

Although almost all Indian lands in Canada are reserves, there are some exceptions. Ownership of some reserves has recently been transferred to individual bands; these reserves are now known as "Band Lands" or lands belonging to a specific group (e.g., Nisga'a Lands).

Also, a negotiated settlement with some Indigenous groups resulted in the 1999 creation of a new federal territory in northern Canada, roughly equivalent to a province in Canada or a state in the United States. Known as **Nunavut**, meaning "Our Land" in the Inuit language of Inuktitut, the territory is substantial. It is about the size of Western Europe, and if it were a country it would be the 15th largest in terms of landmass. Situated in the far North with relatively sparse natural resources, it has one of the lowest population densities in the world. The population is approximately 30,000, with more than 80 per cent identifying as Inuit.

In the US there are multiple kinds of Indian lands. These include trust land (held by the government for the use of Indians) and restricted fee simple lands (allowing Indian ownership, but with limitations on its use and transfer). Some 45 million acres are held in tribal trust with another 10 million in individual Indian trust. Alaska Natives control close to another 100 million acres. In total, Indian lands in the United States comprise about 4 per cent of the country's landmass.

INDIGENOUS PEOPLES OF NORTH AMERICA IN A GLOBAL PERSPECTIVE

The Indigenous peoples of North America have much in common with Indigenous peoples elsewhere. This includes a history of being subjugated by more dominant societies, often by the same means—such as deliberate attempts to crush Indigenous identity, forced assimilation, and in some cases genocide.

The global Indigenous movement began in the late twentieth century, when various groups of Indigenous peoples around the world began recognizing common characteristics, working together to protect their identities and cultures, and often seeking redress on an international stage. The rise of indigenism is commonly seen as having been initiated and developed by Indigenous peoples themselves rather than by federal or international organizations or associations. North American Indigenous groups have been involved in the rise of indigenism, but they are by no means alone. Indigenous groups from Central and South America, Australia, New Zealand, Africa, Asia, and Europe have also been involved. As is happening in North America, Indigenous groups elsewhere are increasingly self-identifying as "Indigenous," with terms such as Natives and Aboriginals falling out of favor.

FIGURE 1.6 Indigenous Leadership at the United Nations. Former Grand Chief of the Assembly of First Nations, Ovide Mercredi, giving a speech in the General Assembly Hall at the United Nations. Indigenous peoples in North America have joined Indigenous peoples elsewhere in bringing their issues to the international stage, such as at the UN. (UN Photo 182273 / E. Debebe. Reprinted by permission.)

While indigenism began with Indigenous peoples themselves, it has become an area of considerable academic interest, and provides a framework through which many researchers now study Indigenous groups. It provides another context, beyond local, regional, national, and continental perspectives, for describing and understanding the histories, and current state of Indigenous peoples in North America.

It is impossible to get an accurate figure of the number of Indigenous peoples worldwide; scholarly estimates usually range between 250 and 600 million. A 2010 estimate by the United Nations suggested that there were about 370 million Indigenous peoples in 90 countries. The North American Indigenous population thus constitutes only about 1 per cent of the total Indigenous population around the world.

The international perspectives on North American Indigenous peoples have focused primarily on the struggle for rights. Because of the broad similarities in colonial histories, North American Indigenous groups are frequently considered on the global scale to be most closely related to the Indigenous groups of Australia and New Zealand.

Despite the global rise of indigenism, the issues of most Indigenous groups in North America, such as health, education, self-government, and rights to land and resources, are only considered on a national level. Bringing such issues to the international stage, such as at the United Nations, is a strategy that may eventually be used to bring a sense of urgency to federal governments—the **politics of embarrassment**.

Such was the case with the adoption of the United Nations Declaration on the Rights of Indigenous People (see Appendix 1). When it was adopted by the United Nations General Assembly in 2007, 143 nations voted in favor of the declaration and only four countries were opposed. Those opposed were Australia, New Zealand, Canada, and the United States. In subsequent years, each of these four countries has reversed its decision, likely due at least in part to the politics of embarrassment.

SUGGESTED READINGS

The popularity of the term Indigenous and the associated Indigenous movement has received considerable attention in recent years. Recommended sources include the website of the United Nations Permanent Forum on Indigenous Issues (www.un.org/esa/socdev/unpfii). One of the leading scholars on the Indigenous movement is Ronald Niezen, whose publications include the book *The Origins of Indigenism: Human Rights and the Politics of Identity* (2005) and a contribution called "The Global Indigenous Movement" in the *Handbook of North American Indians, vol. 2: Indians and Contemporary Society,* edited by Garrick Bailey (2008). Other recommended books include *First Peoples: Indigenous Cultures and Their Futures,* by Jeffrey Sissons (2005), and *The Indigenous Experience: Global Perspectives,* edited by Roger Maaka and Chris Andersen (2006).

Basic data on Indigenous groups can usually be found through links on the web pages of the federal agencies with primary responsibility for those groups. In the United States, this agency is the Bureau of Indian Affairs (www.bia.gov), while in Canada it is Aboriginal Affairs and Northern Development Canada (www.aadnc-aandc.gc.ca). Summaries of data for United States groups can also be found in *The State of Native Nations,* from the Harvard Project on American Indian Economic Development (2008).

Good sources on Indian identity are those by Eva Marie Garroutte and Circe Sturm, especially Garroutte's book *Real Indians: Identity and the Survival of Native America* (2003); her contribution "Native American Identity in Law" in the second volume of the *Handbook of North American Indians* (2008); and Sturm's book focusing on Cherokee identity, *Blood Politics: Race, Culture, and Identity in the Cherokee Nation of Oklahoma* (2002).

TWO

STUDYING THE INDIGENOUS PEOPLES OF NORTH AMERICA THROUGH THE LENS OF ANTHROPOLOGY

Indians have been cursed above all other people in history.
Indians have anthropologists.
–Vine Deloria, Jr., *Custer Died for Your Sins*

And the Anthros still keep on coming
Like death and taxes to our land.
–Floyd Red Crow Westerman, *Here Come the Anthros*

INTRODUCTION

This chapter provides a framework for understanding the Indigenous peoples of North America from an anthropological perspective. It does this by describing what is meant by the anthropological perspective; providing a brief overview of the anthropology of the Indigenous peoples of North America; outlining a critique on the work of anthropologists; and considering this work in a global perspective.

THE ANTHROPOLOGICAL PERSPECTIVE

There are many different definitions of **Anthropology**; Table 2.1 offers three reasonable examples. The key element in all definitions of anthropology is that the focus is on humans. This includes all aspects of human life, including **culture** and biology, past and present.

The most appropriate definition of anthropology often depends on context. When making general distinctions between various academic disciplines or fields of interest, for example, "Anthropology is the study of

TABLE 2.1
Defining Anthropology

Anthropology is the study of humans.

Anthropology is the study of humans, focusing on the description and explanation of human cultures and biology, and including the scholarly collection, analysis, and interpretation of data related to humans, past and present.

Anthropology is the study of humans through evolutionary, comparative, and holistic perspectives.

humans" is often sufficient. Many scholars and professionals outside of anthropology also focus on one or more aspects of humans, however, and some anthropologists prefer to distinguish the discipline based on their focus and methods, leading to such definitions as, "Anthropology is the study of humans, focusing on the description and explanation of human cultures and biology, and including the scholarly collection, analysis, and interpretation of data related to humans, past and present." Other anthropologists tend to make the distinction between anthropology and other scholarly interests in humans by the perspective one takes, leading to such definitions as, "Anthropology is the study of humans through evolutionary, comparative, and holistic perspectives."

Culture is a core concept in anthropology, and may be defined as the learned and shared things that people have, think, and do as members of a society. The things that people have are commonly known as material culture and include things that are tangible, such as tools and structures. The things that people think are often referred to as ideology and include beliefs, morals, and values. The things that people do are commonly called customs and include behavior patterns. Language is usually considered a key component of culture, as well.

All societies have culture. One way of distinguishing between culture and society is to think of society as being comprised of people, and culture as being what binds those people together as a distinct group. There are several thousand distinct cultures recognized around the world today (based on distinct languages). Each of the major Indigenous groups in North America, for example, such as Cherokee, Navajo, Mohawk, and hundreds of others, are considered to be distinct cultures. In the past, there were likely more cultures, both in North America and elsewhere.

Elements of culture need not be mutually exclusive. For example, neighboring Indigenous groups in North America may have many similarities, but differences in language or slight nuances in technology, behavior, and thoughts may be enough to distinguish different cultures.

Culture is learned; it is not instinctive. People are not born with a predisposition to learning a specific language or having particular religious beliefs, for example. Culture is also shared, although not every member of a society necessarily has to share in the material culture, customs, or beliefs. People living in a religious society need not be religious themselves, for example, but religious beliefs will still be part of their culture.

Anthropologists recognize several major components of culture (see Table 2.2). Subsistence refers to the strategies people use to obtain food, such as foraging wild plants, hunting wild animals, herding animals, or farming. Anthropologists are interested in describing and explaining the strategies used by different groups. Related to this is the anthropological interest in documenting the specific foods eaten by different groups and the ways these foods are processed, distributed, and consumed.

The term "settlement patterns" refers to the patterns in which people move about on the landscape, how long they stay in one place, and the size and structure of their settlement sites. Anthropologists are interested in describing and explaining the factors that influence the degree of these groups' mobility, the choice of their locations, and the structure of their settlements.

Technology refers to the way people create material culture. This includes a wide variety of things including tools, structures, and monuments. Technology also refers to the way people process things, such as cooking and preserving foods, or creating visual **art**.

Communication includes language and other forms of expression. Anthropologists study both verbal and non-verbal systems of communication, such as symbols and gestures. They are interested in the structure of languages, the relationship between language and thought, body language, the use of space, social dialects, language change, and the preservation of language.

Economic systems include the modes of production, distribution, trade, and consumption. Anthropologists are interested in documenting and explaining patterns of labor, such as the division of labor between males and females, and occupational specialization. They are also interested in the accumulation and distribution of goods, both within and between groups.

Social and political systems involve a wide variety of things that affect daily living. Anthropologists are particularly interested in the form and function of social organizations based on **descent groups**, **kinship groups**, marriage and family patterns, common interest associations, and social inequality. Anthropologists are also interested in describing and explaining how specific forms of influence, leadership, and government are used to maintain social control within a group and maintain relationships with other groups.

TABLE 2.2
Major Components of Culture

Component	Meaning
Subsistence	How people get their food, and the kinds of food they eat.
Settlement Patterns	How people move and settle on the landscape.
Technology	How people accomplish tasks, such as hunting, cooking, making tools, and building houses.
Communication	How people use language and non-verbal systems to communicate.
Economic Systems	How food and material goods are produced and distributed.
Social Systems	How people organize themselves according to descent, kinship, marriage, class, and other groupings.
Political System	How leadership works and how order is maintained within and between groups.
Ideology	How people relate to the spiritual and supernatural world, as well as values and worldview.
Arts	How people express aesthetics through visual means such as painting, carving, weaving, and sculpture; and through performance such as dancing, singing, creating music, and acting.
Health and Healing	How people diagnose and treat illnesses.

Ideology includes beliefs about the supernatural world and associated rituals. Anthropological interests in ideology focus on the form and function of **mythology**, **shamans**, cosmology, and ceremonial life.

The arts include both visual arts, such as painting and sculpture; and performing arts, such as dance and music.

Health and healing involves general health as well as the treatment of illnesses. Anthropologists focus on changes in health patterns and the distinctions between the recognition and treatment of illnesses determined to be based on physical causes versus those based on spiritual causes.

More in-depth coverage of these major components of culture, as they pertain particularly to the Indigenous peoples of North America, is included in subsequent chapters. Language is covered more comprehensively in Chapter 4; traditional forms of the major components are covered in Chapter 5; and the impacts of colonialism on these components are covered in Chapter 6.

In North America, anthropology is usually considered to have four major branches: **cultural anthropology**, **archaeology**, **biological anthropology**, and **linguistics**.

Cultural anthropology, also known as social anthropology or socio-cultural anthropology, is the largest subfield of anthropology in North America, and is focused on cultures of the present and recent past. Cultural anthropologists typically immerse themselves within a group for an extensive period and then write a description of that group's culture, which is known as an **ethnography**. The principal method of ethnographic research is **participant-observation**. Traditionally, ethnographies have focused on one or more of the components of culture listed in Table 2.2, but recent ethnographies have begun to tackle such things as culture change and identity formulation. Ethnographies provide much of the raw data of cultural anthropology and are often published as books. All major Indigenous groups in North America have had multiple ethnographies written about them.

Archaeology involves the study of past human groups through their material remains, such as discarded tools and the remnants of settlements. Archaeologists in North America usually seek to reconstruct one or more components of the cultures of past groups, and to explain culture change.

Linguistics, also known as linguistic anthropology or anthropological linguistics, focuses on human languages. In studies of North American Indigenous peoples, linguistic research tends to focus on the classification of languages; determining cultural relationships in the past based on the similarities in language; the use of language; and the importance of language to other aspects of culture.

Biological anthropology, also known as physical anthropology, focuses on human biology, past and present. In North America, most biological anthropological research focuses on skeletal remains recovered from archaeological sites. Skeletal evidence has been used to make inferences about many aspects of peoples from the past, including diet, health, and disease. Recently, biological anthropologists have been studying DNA as well, particularly to aid in the determination of ancestral relationships.

Although anthropologists in North America usually specialize in one of the four branches, they often receive training in at least one or two of the others, and most North American colleges and universities promote the four-field approach to anthropology. Thus, a cultural anthropologist working with a contemporary North American Indigenous group will often be familiar with both the language of the people and the archaeology of the region. Likewise, an archaeologist will often have knowledge of ethnographies and be able to excavate and analyze human skeletal remains of living groups, assuming that this is in accord with the wishes of that Indigenous group.

TABLE 2.3
Anthropological Perspectives

Holistic	Considering that all components of a culture are interrelated.
Evolutionary	Considering that cultures are continually changing.
Comparative	Considering the importance of comparison when describing and explaining.
Qualitative	Tendency to focus on qualitative (vs. quantitative) data, especially in ethnography.
Focus on linkages	Recognizing the importance of the links between the components of culture.
Focus on change	Focusing on culture change.
Based on fieldwork	Preference of anthropologists for collecting their own primary data. For ethnography, this usually means participant-observation. For archaeology, this usually means conducting excavations.

Anthropology is certainly not the only academic discipline to study humans. All of the disciplines falling within the realm of the liberal arts, social sciences, or humanities essentially focus on some aspect of human culture. These include, for example, psychology, economics, sociology, political science, human geography, history, philosophy, art history, and literature.

The anthropological perspective distinguishes anthropology from these other disciplines (see Table 2.3). The characteristic that anthropology is best known for is **holism**, or the holistic perspective. In a broad sense, this refers to the recognition in anthropology that on a very broad level, human culture and human biology are linked; but more particularly the holistic perspective is often equated with the idea that all components of a culture are intricately linked. In practical terms, this means that if an anthropologist wants to understand the economy of a culture, for example, he or she must understand that the economy is intricately linked with subsistence strategies, diet, settlement patterns, social and political institutions, ideology, and more. Further, in understanding how and why cultures change, anthropologists appreciate that a change in any single aspect of a culture will inevitably have repercussions in other components of the culture.

It is this recognition of the connections and linkages between components of culture that often distinguishes anthropology, and it provides the focus for much anthropological work. Examples include anthropologists researching the connection between language and hunting; political institutions and belief systems; subsistence strategies and social institutions, and so on.

Comparative and evolutionary approaches also characterize anthropology. The comparative approach is common; it uses information from a wide diversity of studies to explain similarities and differences between groups, past and present. This happens with regularity in the study of North American Indigenous groups, for example, where anthropologists frequently draw on information from a number of ethnographies of a particular group or from a variety of groups living in the same region in order to make some generalizations and offer explanations of cultural phenomena.

The evolutionary approach is based on the notion that a full understanding of cultural traits is often best explained by a long-term evolutionary sequence, supported by archaeological and historic data. This approach is particularly relevant to the study of the Indigenous peoples of North America, where archaeological research indicates that in many areas, the contemporary Indigenous populations can trace their ancestry in the regions for thousands of years. It is perhaps important to note here that in this context, "evolution" roughly equates with "change" and has no attachment to common views held in the late nineteenth and early twentieth centuries by many, including some anthropologists, that societies progressed in a unilinear way through stages until civilization was achieved, and that some Indigenous societies were more evolved than others.

Reliance on fieldwork and qualitative data are other traits that distinguish anthropology. Anthropologists like to collect their own data. For archaeologists this usually means looking for and excavating archaeological sites. For cultural anthropologists, this usually means immersing themselves as much as possible in the culture they are studying. Relying on qualitative data means that anthropologists generally prefer to gather detailed information and insights into a culture based on long-term, firsthand observation, often with the assistance of those from the culture being studied, as opposed to the distribution of surveys to many people over a short period.

A common theme in anthropology is that of adaptation and change. Anthropologists recognize that cultures are continually changing. They are interested in, and investigate, why and how cultures change as people adapt to both the natural environments and to the different societies that they encounter. All cultures are continually changing. They are fluid, rather than static. In North America, this has been true for the cultures of both Indigenous and non-Indigenous peoples.

BRIEF HISTORY OF THE ANTHROPOLOGICAL STUDY OF INDIGENOUS PEOPLES IN NORTH AMERICA

Anthropology emerged as a global academic discipline in the mid-1800s, but scholarly and intellectual interest in the Indigenous peoples of North America emerged considerably earlier. As summarized by anthropologist Alice Kehoe (2006, 556):

... anthropology and American Indians have been in symbiosis even before the emergence of anthropology as a recognized scholarly discipline.... By the eighteenth century, European philosophers such as Rousseau were discussing at length the significance of reported differences between American and European peoples. Weighty questions formulated in those discussions called for directed research that developed through the nineteenth century as the traditionally broad field of philosophy became fragmented into independent disciplines. Observations of American Indians had honed many questions; now scholars would go to American Indian communities to obtain data in greater depth to perhaps answer the questions.

Scholarly research undertaken in the 1700s included the archaeological excavation of a site by Thomas Jefferson, who would later go on to become the third president of the United States. Thousands of large, earthen mounds dotted the landscape in many parts of the eastern United States and there had been much discussion about who had constructed the mounds—was it the ancestors of the contemporary Indigenous peoples or someone else? Jefferson excavated a mound and concluded that, indeed, they had been constructed by the ancestors of the contemporary Indigenous populations.

The thousands of large, earthen mounds continued to be an area of intense interest to many throughout the nineteenth century, and considerable efforts were undertaken to study them before they were destroyed by colonial expansion. The first significant publication on the mounds was *Ancient Monuments of the Mississippi Valley*, by E.G. Squier and E.H. Davis, which came out in 1848 and which was supported by the American Ethnological Society and the Smithsonian Institution.

Anthropology globally emerged as a distinct discipline beginning in the mid-1800s, and many of the most prominent anthropologists of the following 100 years got their foundation by focusing on the Indigenous peoples of North America (see table 2.4). Some remained focused on this area for their entire careers, while others expanded their work to make broader contributions to anthropological theory.

The emergence of anthropology as a scholarly discipline in North America is routinely linked with the work of Lewis Henry Morgan (1818–81). Morgan spent much of his adult life studying Indigenous groups of North America, and the publication of his *League of the Iroqouis* in 1851 is considered a landmark insofar as it is generally recognized as the first scholarly ethnography of any North American Indigenous culture. Morgan also made significant contributions to North American Indigenous systems of **kinship** classification, family, and households.

TABLE 2.4

Some Prominent Figures in the History of North American Anthropology

Lewis Henry Morgan (1818–81)
Morgan is often credited with completing the first scholarly ethnography of a North American Indigenous group (Iroquois), and developing the unilinear theory of cultural evolution.

John Wesley Powell (1834–1902)
Powell headed the Bureau of Ethnology, overseeing many projects on salvage ethnography and archaeology.

Franz Boas (1858–1942)
Boas was the most prominent North American anthropologist in the late 1800s and early 1900s. He countered the unilinear theory of cultural evolution and developed the frameworks of cultural relativism and historical particularism. He undertook considerable fieldwork himself with Indigenous peoples in the Arctic and Pacific Northwest, and oversaw many salvage ethnography and archaeology projects. He taught many of the leading anthropologists of the early twentieth century.

George Hunt (1854–1933)
Hunt was an Indigenous anthropologist who, although formally untrained, collaborated with Boas and other anthropologists on the ethnography of Indigenous peoples for four decades.

Alfred Kroeber (1876–1960)
Kroeber was trained by Boas, and focused on the Indigenous peoples of North America, especially California. He is known, in part, for his association with Ishi.

Robert Lowie (1883–1957)
Lowie achieved his doctorate under the supervision of Boas and became a colleague of Kroeber at the University of California. His dissertation was on the mythology of the Indigenous peoples of North America.

Edward Sapir (1884–1939)
Sapir studied under Boas at Columbia, worked with Kroeber at Berkeley, and headed the Division of Anthropology at the Geological Survey of Canada. He is best known for his work on linguistics, primarily on the languages of the Indigenous peoples of North America.

Diamond Jenness (1886–1969)
Jenness spent several decades on the anthropology of Inuit and First Nations in Canada. For more than two decades he was the head of anthropology at the National Museum of Canada and wrote extensively on both the Inuit and First Nations.

Benjamin Whorf (1897–1941)
Whorf is best known for his studies of languages, particularly with the Hopi, and his work on the relationship between language and thought.

Ruth Benedict (1887–1948)
Benedict studied a variety of Indigenous groups including the Pima, the Pueblo, and the Kwakiutl. Her dissertation was on the concept of guardian spirits among North American Indigenous groups.

Ella Deloria (1888–1977)
Deloria was an Indigenous anthropologist, best known for her book about the Sioux, *Speaking of Indians*, originally published in 1944.

Julian Steward (1902–72)
Steward's dissertation was called *The Ceremonial Buffoon of the American Indian*. Besides his work with the Indigenous peoples of North America, he is well-known for developing the approaches of multilinear evolution and cultural ecology.

Bea Medicine (1923–2006)
Medicine was an Indigenous anthropologist who was widely published and worked in many different institutions throughout the United States and Canada.

The book Morgan is best known for is *Ancient Society or Researches in the Lines of Human Progress from Savagery through Barbarism to Civilization,* published in 1877. Rather than focusing specifically on North American Indigenous peoples, this work was a significant contribution to anthropological theory. In it, Morgan outlined seven stages of human cultural progress, which came to be known as the unilinear or unilineal theory of cultural evolution. Morgan hypothesized that the cultural diversity of living people was evidence that some Indigenous groups around the world were slower to progress and thus were examples of the various stages of savagery and barbarism. According to Morgan's schemes, the Indigenous populations of North America would be viewed as savages and barbarians, and thus inferior to the "civilized" Europeans.

Since Morgan's theory placed Europeans at the pinnacle of human cultural evolution, it was widely accepted by many of those of European descent, and likely justified in their minds their notion of superiority over and exploitation of Indigenous peoples. Much of the anthropological community was not in agreement with the theory, however, and within a few decades it was largely discredited.

While Morgan is often considered to have been the most influential person doing anthropology of North American Indigenous peoples in the mid-1800s, he certainly wasn't alone. Efforts to classify and record languages were ongoing, as was the collection of the material culture of Indigenous peoples. Large museums in Europe started North American Indigenous collections, and many new museums were established in North America that would ultimately create large collections, including the Smithsonian, American Museum of Natural History, and the Canadian Museum of Civilization. Archaeologists and cultural anthropologists were involved in amassing and curating these collections.

The establishment of the Bureau of American Ethnology, often known as the BAE, was an important event in the history of North American anthropology. Initially called the Bureau of Ethnology, it was created in 1879 to collect information on the Indigenous peoples. Led by John Wesley Powell (1834–1902), the BAE undertook large-scale archaeological and ethnographic projects.

Powell and others recognized that the Indigenous cultures were rapidly changing and appreciated the urgency that was required to document the cultures before they either became extinct or underwent significant change. Ultimately this came to be known as **salvage ethnography**, and it dominated much of the anthropological research produced in North America during the late 1800s and early 1900s.

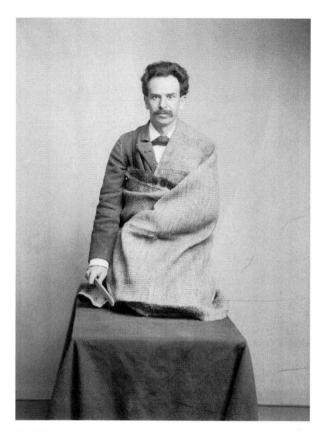

FIGURE 2.1 Franz Boas. He is posing here as a participant in a Kwakiutl ceremony for a museum diorama, 1895. (Photo courtesy of the National Anthropological Archives, Smithsonian Institution MNH 8301.)

From the late 1800s through to the 1940s the most dominant figure in North American anthropology was Franz Boas (1858–1942). As described by Paul Bohannan and Mark Glazer (1988, 81), Boas was "a sort of funnel through which all American anthropology passed between its nineteenth-century juniority and its twentieth-century maturity." Boas was likely the most influential anthropologist in the history of North American anthropology.

Boas spent his formative years in Germany studying physics, math, and geography, and didn't enter the field of anthropology until he had finished university. His dissertation was actually on the color of seawater. His scholarly interest in seawater led him to the Arctic in 1883, and it was his extended stay with the Inuit there that spurred his interest in North

American Indigenous peoples. His interest was further piqued when, back in Germany a few years later, he met a group of visiting Indigenous people from the west coast of Canada (i.e., the Nuxalk, previously known as the Bella Coola Indians). Boas subsequently made many visits to the Pacific Northwest region of the continent and, basing himself out of New York, established himself as the preeminent anthropologist of the late 1800s and early 1900s. His significant accomplishments included many publications on the Indigenous peoples of the continent, especially in the Pacific Northwest; working at the American Museum of Natural History in New York; and establishing the department of anthropology at Columbia University, where he was able to train many subsequent North American anthropologists.

Boas made many contributions to the ethnography, archaeology, linguistics, and biological anthropology of North American Indigenous peoples through his own fieldwork. He was also able to secure funding for massive anthropological projects undertaken by others, and influence the development of anthropology in North America by his emphasis on salvage ethnography and his contributions to anthropological theory.

Significant contributions in this regard include Boas's development of **cultural relativism** (meaning that one component of a society's culture should be explained in relation to other parts of that culture, rather than being evaluated on criteria imposed by others); and **historical particularism** (meaning that each culture is a product of its own unique evolution, and can only be understood in that context). Cultural relativism and historical particularism are particularly important insofar as they countered Lewis Henry Morgan's theory of unilinear evolution.

One cannot underestimate the influence of Franz Boas on the development of North American anthropology. Besides his contributions to the anthropology of the Indigenous peoples of the Arctic and Pacific Northwest; his methodological and theoretical influence (in many cases by direct teaching) on many of the prominent anthropologists of the early 1900s; his countering of the unilinear theory of evolution; and his development of cultural relativism and historical particularism (which remain key notions for many anthropologists), he also is important for developing the four-field approach in North American anthropology (which, unlike many other areas of the world, encourages training in each of cultural anthropology, archaeology, biological anthropology, and linguistics). He is further well-known for his encouragement for women entering the field of anthropology (e.g., Margaret Mead and Ruth Benedict); formally training and collaborating with Indigenous people in anthropology, such as Ella Deloria and George Hunt; and training some of the pre-eminent North American anthropologists of the

---

BOX 2.1

Ishi

Ishi was the name given to an Indigenous person in California who, after spending more than 40 years avoiding contact with Euro-Americans, spent the last five years of his life working closely with anthropologists Alfred Kroeber and T.T. Waterman.

Ishi was probably born in 1864 and lived with a small group, undetected, until he and three other adults were discovered by surveyors in 1908. It is assumed that the three others died soon thereafter and that Ishi decided to stop avoiding Euro-Americans in 1911. Prior to this, many members of his nation had been massacred by Euro-Americans and many others had assimilated into Euro-American society.

Anthropologist Alfred Kroeber arranged for Ishi to live at the museum of the University of California from 1911 until his death from tuberculosis in 1916. Ishi aided anthropologists in documenting his language and culture. He also gave demonstrations of making stone tools, archery, and other technological skills to museum visitors, and worked as a janitor in the museum.

Kroeber and other anthropologists were particularly interested in Ishi since he gave them an opportunity to study an Indigenous person and culture less affected by Europeans than most others. Ishi was widely promoted as "the last wild Indian" and the "last of his tribe." We now know that this was not true. Although he had little direct contact with Euro-Americans prior to 1908, he certainly was aware of them, and European materials were found at one of his last camps. We also now know that his entire group did not become extinct.

Following Ishi's death, his body was autopsied and cremated. His brain was sent to the Smithsonian in 1917 and repatriated to the representatives of his group (the Redding Rancheria and Pit River Tribe) in 2000.

Ishi was not his real name; it was the name for "man" in his own language (Yana). He never spoke his real name.

---

twentieth century, such as Alfred Kroeber, Robert Lowie, and Edward Sapir.

Alfred Kroeber (1876–1960) was the first to achieve a doctorate under Boas, and he became particularly well-known for his work with Indigenous groups in North America, particularly California. He also is associated with Ishi, an Indigenous man from California who became a museum exhibit, and a janitor, in the early 1900s (see Box 2.1).

The relationship between anthropologists and Indigenous peoples in North America has gone through significant changes over the past 150 years. From its beginning, anthropology in North America developed primarily on the basis of studies on the archaeology, ethnography, languages, and biology of the Indigenous peoples of the continent. For much of the history of North American anthropology, the Indigenous peoples were at the center of interest. That seemed to change in the 1960s, and while many anthropologists continue their interest in the Indigenous cultures, those interests are no longer as central to the discipline as they once were. As stated by Orin Starn (2011, 180–81):

FIGURE 2.2 Ishi. Widely promoted as the last wild Indian and the last of his tribe, Ishi was neither. He lived his final years in the Hearst Museum in Berkeley. (Photo by the Phoebe A. Hearst Museum of Anthropology at the University of California, Berkeley. Reprinted by permission.)

At the start, most US anthropologists made their living studying Indians, this almost parasitic disciplinary dependence lasting well into the 20th century. Then came the turmoil of the 1960s and 1970s, the Red Power Movement, and a period of estrangement between anthropologists and Native America…. It can be easy to forget just how central Native Americans once were to US anthropology; Papa Franz and virtually all his students fanned out into Indian country like a second invading army, this time armed with notebooks and seizing not territory but instead information about myths, rituals, and kinship systems.

INDIGENOUS ANTHROPOLOGISTS AND CRITIQUE

Indigenous people of North America have been doing anthropology in their countries since the late 1800s. Ella Deloria (1888–1977) trained and worked with Boas during the early 1900s, focusing on ethnography and language, for example; and George Hunt (1854–1933) collaborated with Boas and others on the ethnography of Pacific Northwest Indigenous groups for more than 40 years. Bea Medicine (1923–2006) was a prominent figure in the mid to late 1900s, working in universities throughout the United States and Canada. Participation in the profession has continued to grow since the mid-1900s, and there are many Indigenous anthropologists in North

FIGURE 2.3 George and Francine Hunt. George collaborated with Franz Boas and other anthropologists on many anthropological projects in the late 1800s and early 1900s. His wife Francine posed for photographer Edward Curtis while he was documenting traditional cultures on the west coast. (Photo courtesy of Royal BC Museum, BC Archives. BCARS AA-00242.)

America today. In 2007, the Association of Indigenous Anthropologists was created within the American Anthropological Association.

Anthropologists' work with Indigenous peoples in North America has been criticized throughout the history of the discipline—sometimes fairly, and sometimes not. Some critics have viewed, and continue to view, anthropology as an agent of colonialism or imperialism, claiming that anthropologists are mere pawns collecting information on Indigenous peoples that may subsequently be used against them. There is a long history, on the other hand, of anthropologists working with and advocating on behalf of Indigenous peoples. Lewis Henry Morgan, for example, was trained as a lawyer and represented the interests of the Seneca, for which he was made an honorary member; and anthropologists spoke out against the Canadian legislation banning the **potlatch.** The often good relations many anthropologists have had with the people they were studying has been reflected in many of them being adopted into these groups, or in the group's recognition of them in other ways, such as with the conferral of special names.

Much criticism has been leveled against anthropologists for taking information from a community, whether ethnological, archaeological, biological, or language-related, and providing little or nothing to the community

---

BOX 2.2
Anthropologists and Other Friends

Vine Deloria Jr. (1933–2005) was an Indigenous scholar well-known for his criticisms of anthropology. This is an excerpt from Chapter 5 ("Anthropologists and Other Friends") of his first book, *Custer Died for Your Sins: An Indian Manifesto.*

INTO EACH LIFE, it is said, some rain must fall. Some people have bad horoscopes; oth-ers take tips on the stock market.... But Indians have been cursed above all other people in history. Indians have anthropologists.

Every summer when school is out a veritable stream of immigrants heads into Indian country.... From every rock and cranny in the East they emerge, as if responding to some primeval fertility rite, and flock to these reservations.

"They" are the anthropologists.... They are the most prominent members of the scholarly community that infests the land of the free, and in the summer time, the home of the braves.

.... The massive volume of useless knowledge produced by anthropologists attempt-ing to capture real Indians in a network of theories has contributed substantially to the invisibility of Indian people today.... Over the years anthropologists have succeeded in burying Indian communities so completely beneath the mass of irrelevant informa-tion that the total impact of the scholarly community on Indian people has become one of simply authority.... The implications of the anthropologist, if not for all of America, should be clear for the Indian. Compilation of useless knowledge "for knowledge's sake" should be utterly rejected by the Indian people ... In the meantime it would be wise for anthropologists to get down from their thrones of authority and PURE research and begin helping Indian tribes instead of preying on them.

---

in return. Often an anthropologist would not even share the results of her or his research with the people he obtained the information from, all the while increasing his or her own status within the profession by sharing the information with colleagues and the public through presentations, schol-arly articles, books, and other means.

Other criticisms leveled at anthropologists include their deliberate mis-representations of Indigenous peoples by avoiding descriptions or discus-sion of the impact of Europeans on Indigenous groups. The ethnographies produced by Boas and others were generally devoid of any reference to European people or materials. Basically, many anthropologists described lifeways of the period prior to the arrival of Europeans, but were presenting them as if that was how these groups were living in the present.

Similar criticisms have been leveled against photographers purportedly documenting Indigenous cultures, the most well-known being Edward Curtis, who starting in the 1880s spent more than four decades document-ing more than 80 groups. Many of his photographs were reproduced in the 20-volume series, *The North American Indians.*

The most well-known critic of North American anthropology was the Indigenous scholar Vine Deloria Jr. (1933–2005). He was a Dakota Sioux and a university professor whose academic interests included law, history, politics, and theology. Being related to well-known Indigenous anthropologists Ella Deloria and Bea Medicine, Deloria understood anthropology. His criticism was focused primarily on the failure of anthropologists to make their research on Indigenous peoples relevant to the very people they were studying. His most well-known criticism of anthropologists was published as Chapter 5 ("Anthropologists and Other Friends") in his book *Custer Died for Your Sins: An Indian Manifesto*, published in 1969. (Before the book came out, the chapter appeared in an issue of *Playboy Magazine*.) An excerpt of the chapter is included in Box 2.2.

The publication of *Custer Died for Your Sins* is seen by many as a turning point in the relations between anthropologists and Indigenous peoples. Of course, the critique offered by Deloria should not be viewed out of context. There were other similar criticisms prior to and contemporaneous with that of Deloria, such as *The Unjust Society* in Canada by Harold Cardinal; and there are the backdrops of the civil rights movement and the rise of Indigenous political and cultural revitalization movements to consider. A well-known song by Indigenous activist and musician Floyd Red Crow Westerman (1969) also came out around the same time. Titled *Here Come the Anthros*, and from an album with the same title as Deloria's manifesto—*Custer Died for Your Sins*—the song includes the following lyrics:

> *And the Anthros still keep coming*
> *Like Death and Taxes to Our Land;*
> *To study their feathered freaks*
> *With funded money in their hand;*
> . . . .
> *Then back they go to write their book*
> *And tell the world there's more;*
> *But there's nothing left to write*
> *It's all been done before*

The anthropological community largely accepted the criticisms by Deloria and others as valid, and it spawned a new era in relations between anthropologists and Indigenous peoples. Indigenous anthropologist Bea Medicine (2001, 3) referred to Deloria's criticisms as "a sweat bath to purge anthropologists of their guilt."

Since the 1970s, the tendency has been for anthropologists to make their work much more relevant to the Indigenous peoples that they work with. Examples include assisting them to document their past and present lifeways for myriad reasons, including preserving disappearing languages

FIGURE 2.4 King Island Village. This Indigenous village in Alaska was photographed by Edward Curtis. Despite criticisms, Curtis's photos provide excellent documentation of Indigenous culture, especially housing. (Photo courtesy of the Library of Congress.)

and other aspects of traditional lifeways; protecting heritage sites; and preparing for negotiating agreements or court cases. In many cases, it is the Indigenous peoples themselves who seek out anthropologists for practical and applied purposes.

Most anthropologists working with Indigenous peoples today are bound by ethical guidelines. Most associations of anthropologists have strict guidelines about how to interact with the groups they work with, recognizing an obligation on the part of anthropologists to those they study. Excerpts from the American Anthropological Association's code of ethics are in Appendix 2.

THE ANTHROPOLOGICAL STUDY OF THE INDIGENOUS
PEOPLES OF NORTH AMERICA IN A GLOBAL PERSPECTIVE
North American anthropology is considerably different than that practiced in most other places around the world. This is likely due to several reasons, including the unique North American history of colonialism, which led to the devastation of Indigenous peoples and cultures at the same time as it generated concerted efforts to document what were perceived to be vanishing cultures. As the discipline of anthropology was emerging, North

America provided a place where anthropologists had what must have appeared to be an enormous supply of cultures to study.

The entire four-field approach of anthropology (combining the branches of cultural anthropology, archaeology, biological anthropology, and linguistics) is primarily a North American phenomenon. In much of the rest of the world, "anthropology" is generally taken to mean what North Americans refer to as cultural anthropology; and other branches are usually recognized as related, but distinct fields of study.

SUGGESTED READINGS

The website for the American Anthropological Association (www.aaanet.org) is useful for a number of reasons. Links can be made from the home page to many areas of potential interest, including "What is Anthropology?"; the association's code of ethics; and the Association of Indigenous Anthropologists.

High Points in Anthropology, second edition, edited by Paul Bohannan and Mark Glazer (1988), includes brief biographies of several prominent anthropologists who worked with North American Indigenous groups. This includes Lewis Henry Morgan, Franz Boas, Alfred Kroeber, Robert Lowie, Edward Sapir, Benjamin Whorf, Ruth Benedict, Ralph Linton, Julian Steward, and Leslie White.

Those interested on the original works of Indigenous anthropologists are directed to Ella Deloria's ([1944] 1998) *Speaking of Indians,* which focuses on the Dakota Sioux; and Bea Medicine's (2001) *Learning to Be an Anthropologist and Remaining Native: Selected Writings.*

A history of the relationships between Indigenous peoples is covered by an article called "Here Come the Anthros (Again): The Strange Marriage of Anthropology and Native America" by Orin Starn (2011). Other good sources include those by Nancy Lurie (1998) and Sergei Kan (2001). For more information on Ishi, see *Ishi in Two Worlds: A Biography of the Last Wild Indian in North America* by Theodora Kroeber (1961) for a broad overview; and Jacknis (2008) for an interesting view on Ishi in the context of museum representation.

Custer Died for Your Sins: An Indian Manifesto by Vine Deloria Jr. ([1969] 1996) is recommended for his criticism of anthropology; and *Indians and Anthropologists: Vine Deloria, Jr., and the Critique of Anthropology,* edited by Thomas Biolsi and Larry J. Zimmerman (1997), is recommended for examples of how it changed anthropology in North America.

THREE

COMPREHENDING NORTH AMERICAN ARCHAEOLOGY

INTRODUCTION

There are many ways of learning about North American **prehistory**, including through the oral traditions of Indigenous peoples. The primary method of learning about the prehistoric human past in North America, however, is through archaeology.

Following a brief description of Indigenous versus archaeological concepts of time, this chapter provides an overview of the nature of archaeology as it is practiced in North America in the early twenty-first century. This, in turn, is followed by an outline of North American prehistory, a short section on the archaeology of the colonial period, and a discussion of North American archaeology and prehistory in a global perspective.

CONCEPTS OF TIME

There are several distinct views of time, including its nature and importance. Most non-Indigenous peoples, including archaeologists, generally follow the notion that time is linear and can be measured accurately. Many Indigenous peoples, on the other hand, have different views of time, including such ideas as that it may be cyclical; that there may be little distinction between past and present when it comes to the mythological world; and the belief that time is immeasurable. This isn't to say that Indigenous peoples aren't timely or that they necessarily reject non-Indigenous emphases on precise measurements. Rather, as a generalization, Indigenous peoples tend not to put as much importance on the precise dates of past events as non-Indigenous peoples do.

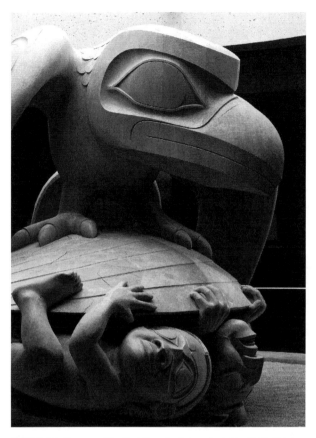

FIGURE 3.1 Raven and the First Men. Sculpture depicting Haida Origin Myth with Raven coaxing the first humans out of a giant clamshell. (Sculpture by Haida artist Bill Reid. Photo by Goh Iromoto. Photo courtesy of UBC Museum of Anthropology.)

Indigenous scholar Vine Deloria Jr., in his book *God is Red* (2003, 97), describes the differences between Indigenous and non-Indigenous concepts of time as follows:

> The western preoccupation with history and a chronological description of reality was not a dominant factor in any tribal conception of either time or history. Indian tribes had little use for recording past events; the idea of keeping a careful chronological record of events never seemed to impress the greater number of tribes of the continent.... "The way I heard it" or "it was a long time ago" usually prefaces any Indian account of past tribal experiences, indicating that the story itself is important, not its precise chronological location.

All Indigenous cultures have myths that place their origins a very long time ago, without specifying a particular number of years. It is not uncommon for Indigenous peoples to claim that they have been in their lands forever, or since **time immemorial**. The precise dates are not important. Details of origin stories vary from group to group, but they generally involve a supernatural entity widely known as "The Creator." Groups also commonly have stories explaining how the customs, values, languages, and other phenomena of both the natural and cultural worlds originated, but the precise timing is largely irrelevant in these Indigenous myths. Overall, the Indigenous stories of prehistoric North America rarely focus on time except in very vague ways. And while the stories often explain the origin of both cultural and natural phenomena, they often include supernatural phenomena (as do origin stories of all religions), and so there is little that can be verified by scientific research, including archaeology.

Archaeologists tell a different story about prehistoric North America; a story filled with precise dates and physical evidence. Archaeological stories and Indigenous stories, however, do not necessarily have to be seen in conflict. The generalities of Indigenous stories may often be correlated with the specifics of archaeological research. Many Indigenous stories of the distant past, for example, recall times when there were great bodies of water and unusually large animals where none now exist. It may be that these stories are describing ancestors living among the mammoths, mastodons, and large lakes created by melting glaciers more than 10,000 years ago, of which there is considerable tangible evidence.

THE NATURE OF NORTH AMERICAN ARCHAEOLOGY

What Constitutes the Archaeological Record of North America?

The archaeological record of prehistoric North America comprises the physical evidence of people's activity left during the prehistoric time period. The major kinds of evidence are outlined in Table 3.1.

Despite the impact of people on the landscape in recent times, hundreds of thousands of **archaeological sites** and millions of **artifacts** have been recorded by archaeologists working in North America. At least that many more are likely to exist, as of yet undiscovered and unrecorded.

An archaeological site may be broadly defined as any location where there is physical evidence of past human activity. Settlements are one of the most important kinds of archaeological sites. Some, such as those with houses made of **adobe,** can remain visible for a thousand or more years (e.g., see Figure 1.4, Taos Pueblo). **Tipi** villages can often be identified by the rings of stone that they leave behind, which were used to hold the rim

TABLE 3.1

Principal Constituents of the Archaeological Record of Prehistoric North America

Archaeological Sites
In general, an archaeological site is any location where there is physical evidence of human activity. In North America, there are hundreds of thousands of documented archaeological sites dating to the time before Europeans arrived. These include settlements, rock art, and burial grounds.

Artifacts
Artifacts are portable objects with physical evidence that they have been manufactured, modified, or used by humans. There are many millions of recorded artifacts, including spear and arrow points, pottery, and jewelry.

Features
Features are non-portable objects or patterns that have been manufactured, modified, or used by humans. They include fire hearths, earthworks, middens, and structures.

Plant and Animal Remains
Many archaeological sites contain evidence of plant and animal remains that were used by people, providing considerable information on diet, material culture, and technology.

of the tipi cover to the ground. These are known as **tipi rings**. Many other kinds of houses had foundations dug into the ground which remain discernable to archaeologists long after the structure itself has disappeared. Structures that used poles (e.g., see Figure 2.4) are often discernable as well, for over time the poles will have changed the color and consistency of the ground they were in. Archaeologists often refer to these as post holes, and can use them to determine the size, shape, and number of houses in a village. Discrete accumulations of trash associated with villages are commonly known as **middens**, and these are a common place for archaeologists to excavate, considering the quantity of cultural material likely to be recovered there. When the middens contain fragments of shell, they are usually referred to as **shell middens**; these are commonly found in coastal areas and along inland river systems where shellfish comprised part of the local diet.

Other major kinds of sites include rock art sites. These include both **pictographs** (paintings on rock outcrops) and **petroglyphs** (carvings on rock outcrops); sites where people manufactured stone tools and pottery; sites where people built structures to assist in hunting or fishing, such as hunting blinds; and sites where people processed and stored their foods, including locations of butchering, cooking, smoking, and drying.

Artifacts may be broadly defined as any portable object that exhibits physical evidence of being manufactured, modified, or used by people. The

FIGURE 3.2 Artifacts and Ecofacts. Potsherds, stone tools, plant remains, and animal bones, such as these recovered at Ute Mountain Tribal Park in Colorado are the primary kinds of remains that archaeologists use to reconstruct past lifeways. (Photo © Barry D. Kass@ ImagesofAnthropology.com. Reprinted by permission.)

most common types of artifacts recovered from prehistoric sites in North America are made of stone or clay. Stone tools often include complete or broken **projectile points**. Clay artifacts are usually broken pieces of pottery, known as **potsherds**. Archaeologists recognize that there is a bias towards inorganic artifacts in the archaeological record, since they preserve much better than organic remains. It is clear, however, that although most artifacts that preserve are made of stone or clay, many cultures in the past relied heavily on artifacts made from organic materials such as wood, plant fibers, bone, and shell. The prehistoric site of Ozette on the coast of Washington State provides an excellent example of a group's reliance on organic artifacts. This particular site was buried by a mudslide, effectively preserving the organic remains. Tens of thousands of artifacts were recovered, with well over 90 per cent being made from organic material.

Plant and animal remains found in archaeological sites are often called **ecofacts.** Archaeologists commonly use them to reconstruct past environments and diets. Sometimes, if they are found outside of the areas where they naturally occur, ecofacts can also be used to make inferences about interactions between groups, including trade.

One of the ways archaeologists attempt to make sense of the vast quantities of data they collect is the assignment of dates to the things they find (i.e., sites, artifacts, and other remains). The principal way archaeologists do this is through **radiocarbon dating,** also known as carbon 14 or C14 dating. The basic principal of the technique is that all living things contain a specific amount of carbon 14, in the same relative proportion. At the instant of death, the carbon 14 begins to decay at a known rate. Therefore, all an archaeologist has to do is determine how much carbon 14 is left in a dead organism and that will lead them to the date at which the organism died. This technique is considered to be very effective, and can be used to date anything found in an archaeological site that was once alive. Commonly dated items include burned wood from **fire hearths** and animal bones. Dates obtained from this technique can be applied to other items in association with the material being dated. A stone arrowhead, for example, may be assigned the same date as a piece of bone or charred wood from a fire if the arrowhead was found in association with that bone or charred wood.

Kinds of Archaeology

There are four major kinds of archaeology being practiced in North America during the early twenty-first century: academic archaeology, CRM archaeology, Indigenous archaeology, and amateur archaeology.

Academic archaeology is based primarily out of universities, and projects are usually focused on pure research. Typically, a professor or student working on a graduate degree (i.e., master's or PhD) develops a project idea that will contribute to furthering the process of documenting or understanding the human past in North American prehistory, which then leads to looking for and/or excavating archaeological sites in order to test a hypothesis. It is mostly academic archaeologists that interpret the data comprising the archaeological record to create views of local, regional, and continental **culture history**, and to explain the major events of the past. The primary objective of academic archaeology projects is to better understand the human past of North America, and it is mostly the results of academic archaeology projects that are presented at conferences, are described and discussed in articles published in the scholarly and popular presses, provide the basis for documentary films on archaeology, and are featured in news stories about archaeology.

In the 1960s and 1970s a new kind of archaeology emerged, now known as **Cultural Resource Management**—often abbreviated **CRM**. CRM refers to archaeology being done before, or at the same time as, development projects that have the potential to destroy known and unknown archaeological sites. This typically involves looking for and recording sites in an area slated for development before it occurs, and then excavating those sites in advance of the development if they are deemed significant. In many cases, governments insist that developers hire archaeologists to undertake an archaeological impact assessment on any land that will be altered, and if determined by the government to be appropriate, to excavate significant sites that would otherwise be destroyed by the development. This is the dominant form of archaeology being practiced in North America during the early twenty-first century. The primary objective of CRM is to simply collect data before the evidence is lost through development. In this regard, CRM archaeology is much like the salvage ethnography that characterized ethnographic research in the late nineteenth and early twentieth centuries; in fact, in its early years (1960s and 1970s) it was commonly known as "salvage archaeology." Vast quantities of data are accumulated through CRM, with many thousands of sites and artifacts continuing to be discovered and recorded. In most cases, however, the information remains contained within reports that are on file with government agencies. Much of the primary data on prehistoric North America is contained within the hundreds of thousands of these reports. The National Archaeological Database (NADB) includes about 350,000 archaeological reports. On occasion, some of the data collected by CRM archaeologists will be used by academic archaeologists, but when CRM archaeology is in the news it most often remains local and in the context of something being discovered that may impede development.

The late twentieth and early twenty-first centuries saw the emergence of Indigenous archaeology, which can be broadly defined as archaeology that is informed by and incorporates Indigenous agendas, knowledge, and perspectives. Objectives of Indigenous archaeology projects include, but are not limited to, providing support for claims of rights and territory; providing documentation of a group's past for cultural reasons; and managing their own resources. Both Indigenous and non-Indigenous archaeologists are involved in Indigenous archaeology. Indigenous archaeology includes components of both academic and CRM archaeology, so in addition to collecting data for an Indigenous group's own purposes, Indigenous archaeologists often write for academic and general audiences as well.

Amateur archaeology comes in two primary forms. One is that of volunteers following the methods of archaeology under the guidance of professional archaeologists. The other form is that of people who destroy archaeological sites while searching for artifacts as a hobby or for profit. These types of people are often referred to as looters or **pothunters**. Those who volunteer on projects under the direction of professional archaeologists provide a valuable service and are often welcomed. In some cases,

BOX 3.1
Rudy Reimer/Yumks—Indigenous Archaeologist

FIGURE 3.3 (Photo courtesy of Rudy Reimer/Yumks.)

Rudy Reimer, also known by his Indigenous name of Yumks, is a member of the Squamish Nation of the Coast Salish group, whose traditional territories lay in the Pacific Northwest region of North America.

Rudy is one of many Indigenous people to enter the fields of anthropology in recent years, and who have achieved PhDs and incorporated Indigenous perspectives into their research, writing, and teaching. He teaches in both the department of archaeology and the department of First Nations studies at Simon Fraser University in Canada, and often undertakes archaeological fieldwork in the traditional territory of the Squamish Nation. His principal interests include bringing Indigenous theory into academic studies, integrating Indigenous perspectives into archaeological interpretation, identifying Indigenous social and ideological values in relation to archaeological sites, and working with Indigenous groups in land and resource planning.

projects depend on these volunteers. Those who loot archaeological sites, on the other hand, pose a great problem. Someone looking to collect artifacts as a hobby or for profit can destroy the integrity of an archaeological site very quickly. A site that an archaeologist may take months or years to excavate due to the necessity of accurate record-keeping can be totally destroyed by looters or pothunters in a few hours, rendering useless any further information that comes from that site. Where the primary objective of pothunters is often the finding of artifacts, the goals of archaeologists tend to be very different, with the discovery and analysis of artifacts as simply a method of achieving their broader goals (e.g., determining past lifeways). The context of an artifact—knowing its precise location of discovery and knowing exactly what it was found in association with—is fundamentally important for archaeologists. An artifact out of context, or discovered without reliable record-keeping, is of very limited use to an archaeologist.

TABLE 3.2

Key Legislation Governing Archaeology in the United States and Canada

UNITED STATES

Antiquities Act (1906)
This act established the protection of archaeological sites on federal lands and the permit system for undertaking archaeological investigations.

National Historic Preservation Act (1966)
This act established that archaeological investigations should occur in advance of potential disturbances to federal lands or other lands that may be disturbed by a federally funded project.

Archaeological and Historic Preservation Act (1974)
This act established that federal agencies are responsible for any damage they cause to archaeological sites.

Archaeological Resources Protection Act (1979)
The act established penalties of up to $100,000 and five years in jail for illegal excavations.

The Native Americans Graves Protection and Repatriation Act (1990)
The act established that Indigenous groups will have control and ownership of any human remains and associated artifacts discovered since 1990; and further established that all skeletal and associated objects collected before 1990 must be returned to their Indigenous groups upon request.

CANADA

Provincial and Territorial legislation
Primary responsibility for archaeology is under provincial and territorial jurisdiction, with each province and territory having its own regulations and penalties.

Federal legislation
Archaeological sites on federal lands are protected by the Indian Act (1985), National Parks Act (2000), the Historic Sites and Monuments Act (1985), and the Canadian Environmental Assessment Act (1992).

Legislation

There are several government acts protecting archaeological sites and controlling archaeological research in the United States and Canada (see Table 3.2). Laws vary depending on jurisdiction, but in most cases archaeological sites and artifacts are protected by legislation. In most circumstances, unless one has a permit issued by a government authority (which usually requires at least a master's degree in archaeology or a related discipline, as well as considerable experience), it is illegal to disturb an archaeological site. This does not apply to private property in the United States, but the penalties for looting or otherwise disturbing archaeological sites on public lands can be severe, and often include fines and jail time.

The United States Native American Graves Protection and Repatriation Act (**NAGPRA**) was enacted in 1990 (see Appendix 3). It calls for consultation between archaeologists and Indigenous groups when human remains are found or are expected to be found during excavations; and establishes that ownership and control of human remains and associated objects found since 1990 lies with their affiliated Indigenous groups. The Act further states that all human remains and associated objects that were collected before 1990 must be returned to their affiliated groups upon request. The inventory of human skeletons and associated burial remains collected before 1990 and stored in museums, research institutions, and government agencies includes the bones of more than 150,000 individuals and approximately 2 million funerary artifacts. More than 100,000 sets of skeletal remains and about 1 million associated artifacts remain "culturally unaffiliated," which means that the Indigenous groups to which they should be returned, if requested, is unclear.

There are differing opinions on NAGPRA within the anthropological community. Many—probably most—support NAGPRA, accepting that when it comes to human remains, the values and wishes of the affiliated Indigenous peoples take priority over the wishes of scientists. Those who oppose NAGPRA, on the other hand, tend to believe that when it comes to the remains for which affiliation is uncertain, the pursuit of knowledge by scientists outweighs the interests of Indigenous peoples.

A flashpoint in the interest and debate about NAGPRA occurred with the 1996 discovery of the human remains known as Kennewick Man near Kennewick, Washington. An archaeologist who was also working as a coroner initially used the term "Caucasoid" to describe some of the remains' skeletal features, which led to the suggestion that they likely belonged to someone of European descent. It was subsequently determined that the bones were approximately 9,000 years old—which, since they had previously been described as Caucasoid, created considerable interest among anthropologists and the general public. Following NAGPRA, four different Indigenous groups claimed cultural affiliation with Kennewick Man, requesting that the remains be turned over to them. Some anthropologists were part of a group that decided to take the matter to court, arguing that the remains should not be turned over to the Indigenous groups since cultural affiliation could not be proved. The courts determined that the remains did not meet statutory guidelines in the law, and rather than turn the remains over to the Indigenous groups, they have allowed anthropologists to study them in a court-appointed neutral repository (the Burke Museum in Washington State). Today, most anthropologists believe that Kennewick Man is indeed Native American and that the initial description of "Caucasoid" was unfortunate (especially since this is primarily a racial term, and few anthropologists accept race as a valid biological concept). While Kennewick Man's skeletal features led some to describe him as Caucasoid, his features were not outside the range of variability within Indigenous peoples of North America, past and present.

Discoveries of human remains do not always put archaeologists and Indigenous peoples in conflict; often, archaeologists and Indigenous peoples work together to the satisfaction of all. For example, following the discovery of human remains and associated artifacts that were exposed by a melting glacier in the Pacific Northwest in 1999, there was an immediate meeting of local Indigenous groups, archaeologists, and government officials. The individual was named "Kwayday Dan Ts'inchi," which means "Long Ago Person Found" in the language of one of the local Indigenous groups. The Indigenous groups of the region where he was found, including those of British Columbia, the Yukon, and Alaska, agreed to let the anthropologists study him for a period, and more than 200 Indigenous people underwent DNA testing to assist these studies. After the study was concluded, the remains were returned to the Indigenous peoples, who subsequently had a ceremonial cremation and returned the remains to the glacier.

OUTLINE OF NORTH AMERICAN PREHISTORY

The Initial Peopling of North America

There is a general consensus among archaeologists that people first came to North America during the latter stages of the last ice age, and that North America was populated before Mesoamerica and South America. However, although archaeologists agree that people have been in North America for more than 14,000 years, and most believe that they entered from Asia via the area of the present-day Bering Strait, the questions of precisely when the first migrants arrived and what route they took is subject to debate. In the anthropological community, the general topic is widely known as the "Peopling of the Americas."

A primary challenge for archaeologists has been to explain how the initial migrants got past the glaciers that covered most of Canada at the time of their entry into the country. A variety of hypotheses have been proposed. The two best known are the ice-free corridor hypothesis and the coastal migration hypothesis.

Both the ice-free corridor and the coastal migration hypotheses suggest that the initial people of North America have ancestral ties to Siberia, and that their route was via **Beringia**, also known as the Bering Land Bridge. While most of Canada and much of northern Europe and Asia were under ice during the last ice age, Beringia was a large, ice-free area connecting northeast Asia with north-west North America. Paleoenvironmental research

FIGURE 3.4
Possible Entry Routes to North America during the Latter Stages of the
Last Ice Age

A From north-east Asia, via coastal
margins of Beringia

B From north-east Asia, via interior
Beringia and ice free corridor

C From Europe, via the north Atlantic

Ice Sheet

in Beringia indicates that there were plenty of plant and animal resources suitable for supporting human populations during the last ice age.

The ice-free corridor hypothesis is based on the knowledge that at various times during the last ice age Canada was covered by two large ice sheets. The southern extent of the ice was approximately along the current border between Canada and the United States. One sheet covered most of the area west of the Rocky Mountains and the other sheet covered the area east of the Rocky Mountains. During most of the last ice age, the ice sheets were joined, but during warming trends they separated, providing an ice-free corridor. Proponents of the ice-free corridor hypothesis suggest that peoples from north-east Asia first expanded their territory into Beringia, and then when the corridor was open they simply migrated down it, likely following the large animals they had been depending upon in Asia and Beringia. Paleoenvironmental evidence suggests this route was possible, but there are no widely accepted archaeological sites in the ice-free corridor that are older than 12,000 years. Despite the lack of sites in the corridor, however, this hypothesis remains the traditional archaeological explanation of how people got past the ice sheets during the last glaciations.

The coastal migration hypothesis suggests that rather than depending on large herd animals, the earliest migrants had a **maritime adaptation** and simply followed the coastline, skirting the southern margins of Beringia and then down the west coast of North America until they got past the ice sheet. Some variants of this hypothesis suggest that the earliest migrants would have required boats, but others suggest that since the glaciers did not cover all the land in coastal regions, it may have been possible to maintain foot travel. Paleoenvironmental evidence suggests this route was possible (e.g., locations with abundant plant and animal resources dated between 18,000–16,000 years ago have been found along the coast), but as with the ice-free corridor, no undisputed archaeological sites have been found along the coastal route that are older than 12,000 years. For much of the twentieth century it was thought by many that there were little, if any, locations of plant and animal life on the coast, making the theory unviable. Over the past few decades, however, there are increasing amounts of paleoenvironmental research supporting the idea. Although no sites dated before 12,000 years have been found along the route, there is considerable evidence that the earliest occupants of the west coast, ranging from Alaska to California, were already maritime-adapted immediately following deglaciation.

A third hypothesis to explain how people first arrived in North America, the Solutrean hypothesis, suggests that rather than looking for an Asian ancestry, perhaps the first migrants came from Europe via the north Atlantic Ocean. "Solutrean" is the name of a culture that was present in Europe approximately 20,000 years ago. This hypothesis would have necessitated boat travel across the north Atlantic and then down past the periglacial environment of eastern Canada.

Most archaeologists are inclined to favor either the ice-free corridor or coastal migration routes over the Solutrean hypothesis. This is primarily due to the biological similarities between northeast Asian and North American Indigenous populations; and to the general similarities in cultural attributes, especially stone tool technology, between the cultures of north-east Asia in the range of 20,000–10,000 years ago, the earliest sites in Beringia, and the earliest sites in north-western North America. Most archaeologists do not accept the similarities in stone tool technology between some people living in Europe 20,000 years ago and the earliest inhabitants of North America as being convincing enough to prefer the Solutrean hypothesis.

From 14,000 to 5,000 years ago

There are many thousands of archaeological sites in North America older than 5,000 years. Some of these are shown in Figure 3.5 and described in Table 3.3.

Although there are claims of archaeological sites in North America that are older than 14,000 years, these sites are not widely accepted by archaeologists because (i) they are not indisputably cultural, such as with evidence of so-called artifacts that could be natural; and/or (ii) the dating is not reliable, such as with potential contamination of radiocarbon dates or the use of less-reliable techniques.

Reliably dated archaeological sites start appearing as far back as 14,000 years ago in the archaeological record. Sites from this very early time remain few in number, however, which is at least in part due to a low population density in the first few thousand years of human occupation in North America. The identification of archaeological sites dating to these early years is also problematic. The environments of 14,000 years ago, including coastlines, are significantly different than they are today; sites along coastlines of that time period, for example, are likely to now be underwater. Many thousands of years of natural and cultural phenomena and human activity have likely destroyed many sites, and the kind of things that the earliest populations were doing (e.g., generalized foraging, temporary camps) are not the kinds of things that leave obvious evidence to be found many thousands of years later.

Despite the problems with archaeological visibility, there are some archaeological sites that are widely accepted to be close to 14,000 years

TABLE 3.3

Significant Archaeological Sites in North America Older than 5,000 Years

Bluefish Caves

Located in present-day Yukon territory, Bluefish Caves is significant because it provides evidence of people in Beringia during the last ice age. The site contains artifacts made of stone and bone as well as butchered animal remains. Most archaeologists accept dates between 15,000–12,000 years ago for this site, although some suggest dates in the range of 25,000 years ago.

Cactus Hill

This site is located in Virginia. It is widely accepted as being older than 12,000 years, but the precise antiquity is uncertain. Some suggest that the site may be as old as 17,000–19,000 years, but these older dates are contested.

Gault

This site, located in Texas, was a Clovis camp, and was likely first occupied at least 12,000 years ago. The assemblage includes more than 1 million artifacts overall, including several hundred thousand that are more than 9,000 years old. The site is particularly significant for showing the diversity of diet, which, contrary to popular belief, indicates that mammoths and other large game were only a small part of the Clovis diet. The site is also significant in providing what may be the oldest art in North America, in the form of more than 100 incised stones.

Meadowcroft

Meadowcroft Rockshelter, located in Pennsylvania, is widely considered to contain deposits that are at least 12,000 years old. Some suggest that the deposits may be as old as 19,000 years, but these older dates are contested.

Paisley Cave

Located in Oregon, the oldest deposits in this site contain many human coprolites dated to between 13,000 and 14,000 years ago.

Topper

This site, located in South Carolina, is widely considered to be at least 12,000 years old. Some suggest deposits at the site with artifacts may be considerably older, but there is some question about whether the so-called artifacts from the earlier time periods are really artifacts.

Charlie Lake Cave

This site, located in northern British Columbia, dates to almost 11,000 years ago and would have been in the ice-free corridor. The oldest levels contain, among other things, a fluted point, a stone bead, and bones of several kinds of animals, including bison. DNA analysis of the bison and general similarities in artifacts with earlier sites in Montana suggest movement through the corridor went from south to north.

Daisy Cave

Located on San Miguel Island, about 40 kilometers off the coast of California, this site dates to almost 11,000 years ago. It is particularly significant insofar as it provides early evidence of basketry and cordage, as well as circumstantial evidence of watercraft.

Kennewick

Located in Washington State, this is where the infamous Kennewick Man was discovered. Initially described as Caucasoid and subsequently dated to about 9,000 years ago, the discovery of the remains created considerable debate, both about the initial classification of the remains as Caucasoid and the following controversy about whether the remains should be turned over to Indigenous groups or kept for studies by scientists.

FIGURE 3.5
Significant Archaeological Sites Mentioned in the Chapter

old. Meadowcroft Rockshelter in Pennyslvania, for example, has long been proposed to date back as much as 19,000 years or longer. Although some archaeologists accept the early dates, many do not. Most, however, do accept that the site is at least 12,000 years old. As well, Paisley Cave in Oregon dates to close to 14,000 years ago. The primary evidence from this site comes from **coprolites**, which have provided radiocarbon dates as well as considerable evidence of diet.

A particular way of making projectile points emerged about 12,000 years ago. The technique is known as fluting, which involves removing a channel from the base of the point. Known as the **Fluted Point Tradition**, and encompassing well-known variants such as **Clovis** and **Folsom**, the tradition lasted until about 9,000 years ago and extended from Canada to Mesoamerica. There is strong evidence that the points were used primarily to kill large animals such as mammoths and mastodons, including the discovery of points embedded in their bones.

There is some debate about the specific function of the channel in **fluted points**. Some suggest that it was designed for easier or better hafting to a spear shaft. Others suggest that the channel allowed for more blood loss from an animal once the animal was hit (e.g., blood would pour down the channel, leading to quicker and more blood loss than if speared by other kinds of points).

Although it is evident that peoples of Clovis and other cultures with fluted point technology had a subsistence base that included mammoths, mastodons, and other large animals, there is some uncertainty regarding how important the large animals were. Research at the Gault site, a Clovis period site in Texas, for example, indicates that the people living there had an extremely varied diet.

Fluted point technology disappeared about 9,000 years ago, perhaps resulting from the extinction of mammoths, mastodons, and other large game animals. At one time the extinction of these animals was blamed on overhunting by people but it is now widely thought that the extinctions were more likely due to environmental changes.

It is apparent that the population density of North America increased significantly with the emergence of fluted point technology, likely due at least in part to the ability to effectively hunt big-game animals. Archaeologists aren't certain, however, whether a pre-existing population such as those occupying Paisley Cave and Meadowcroft developed the fluted point technology themselves, which then would have rapidly spread among other populations through **diffusion**; whether a single group living in North America developed the technology and then replaced the populations elsewhere; or whether the introduction of fluted point technology came from a separate migration of people to the Americas 12,000 years ago.

As a generalization it is fair to say that most Indigenous peoples in North America before 5,000 years ago were **foragers**, depending on a diverse array of plants and animals for subsistence. They would have likely been organized as bands, lived in groups of a few dozen or more, and been fairly mobile within an established territory. Groups likely divided when they reached a population of about 50, colonizing adjacent territories. There would have been few limits on population growth and considerable friendly interaction between neighboring bands within a region. Marriage partners would have come from neighboring groups; trade between groups would have occurred; and there would have likely been multiple times during the year when groups got together for economic, social, or ceremonial reasons.

As generalized foragers, each small group likely operated independently, but they would also have identified with distinct ethnic groups (sharing the same language and culture) and had frequent occasion to interact with other groups for economic and social reasons.

From the earliest times, people had sophisticated cultures and were adept at working with stone, wood, bone, animal skins, and fibers. It is almost certain the earliest occupants of the land could make fire. Those in coastal areas were efficiently maritime adapted, including having watercraft and the ability to effectively hunt sea mammals; and many groups were efficient big-game hunters, with the ability to bring down elephant-sized mammoths and mastodons.

The Last 5,000 Years

There are many thousands of important archaeological sites dating to the last 5,000 years of North American prehistory. Several sites are recognized by the United Nations as world heritage sites, putting them in the same category as such well-known attractions as Stonehenge, the Acropolis of Ancient Greece, and the Egyptian pyramids. Some of the most significant sites are described in Table 3.4.

Groups in many areas of the continent continued to rely on foraging as they organized as bands through the last 5,000 years of prehistory, since that was probably what made most sense from an ecological perspective.

Some groups, however, while continuing to depend on wild plants and animals, became increasingly focused on other key resources, and as a result many aspects of their cultures changed. Beginning about 5,000 years ago in the Pacific Northwest, for example, people began to effectively harvest salmon and other marine resources in such abundance that it very

TABLE 3.4

Significant Archaeological Sites in North America Less than 5,000 Years Old

Cahokia
Cahokia, located near St. Louis, is a United Nations World Heritage Site. With an estimated population of about 20,000 people, it was probably the largest prehistoric settlement north of Mexico. The site is an excellent example of the mound-building peoples
from the prehistoric period. Cahokia itself contains more than 100 distinct mounds. The
largest is estimated to have covered 12 acres and been close to 100 feet in height.

Head-Smashed-In Buffalo Jump
This site, located in Alberta, is another United Nations World Heritage Site. It contains
cultural deposits ten meters thick, containing projectile points and buffalo bones. The
site was used for several thousand years, and includes drive lanes to direct buffalo over
the cliff. The site provides considerable evidence of technological and social evolution
related to the communal hunting of buffalo, which was fundamentally important to the
Indigenous peoples of the North American plains and prairies.

Kwayday Dan Ts'inchi
Located in the Pacific Northwest, close to the intersecting borders of Alaska, British
Columbia, and the Yukon, this site yielded an extremely well-preserved body of an
Indigenous man that was exposed by a melting glacier. Studies were undertaken on a
collaborative basis with Indigenous groups and archaeologists, after which the remains
were returned to the land with an Indigenous ritual.

L'Anse aux Meadows
Located in Newfoundland, and a United Nations World Heritage Site, L'Anse aux
Meadows is known best as a Viking settlement dating to about AD 1000. It is the oldest reliably dated site created by Europeans on the continent, but was probably only
used for a few years. The Vikings did not appear to have good relations with Indigenous
peoples in Newfoundland or with Inuit from the same time period in Greenland. The site
was occupied by Indigenous peoples up to 6,000 years ago.

Mesa Verde
Mesa Verde National Park is yet another United Nations World Heritage Site, representative of peoples and cultures of the American Southwest from several hundred to more
than a thousand years ago. The park protects more than 4,000 archaeological sites,
including 600 cliff dwellings constructed mostly with sandstone blocks and adobe mortar.

Ozette
Ozette is a late prehistoric site in Washington State, sometimes referred to as the
"Pompeii of North America" due to the excellent preservation of remains caused by a
catastrophic event. The site consists of a village that was buried by mudslides, preserving several large multi-family houses and tens of thousands of wood and bone artifacts
that would not normally preserve.

quickly led to a growth in population density, the appearance of larger
and more permanent villages, and an increasing complexity in social and
political organization. There is no consensus on why this started to occur
about 5,000 years ago. Some believe it was only then that salmon and other
marine resources became available in the numbers they did, while others
believe that it was linked to the development of harvesting and/or processing technology. Similar occurrences were happening elsewhere, focusing

FIGURE 3.6 Cliff Dwellings at Mesa Verde. (Photo © Barry D. Kass@ImagesofAnthropology. com. Reprinted by permission.)

on different resources. In California, for example, groups began to specialize in acorns.

Elsewhere, especially in the eastern part of the continent from southern Ontario to the Gulf Coast, as well as in the American Southwest (e.g., Arizona, New Mexico), groups began to farm, focusing on crops such as maize, beans, and squash. The reasons that people started farming are unclear. Anthropologists are generally aware that in most circumstances, and for most people, a lifeway dependent on domestic plants requires more work than one dependent on game, and health often suffers in the transition. In any event, farming created a surplus which in turn supported, and perhaps led to, larger populations, increased sedentism, and more complex social and political organization.

Mostly, it was plants that were domesticated. It is widely assumed that dogs were domesticated at least several thousand years ago, probably to assist in hunting and for protection. They may also have been prestige items or pets. Although they were occasionally eaten, it is unlikely that they were bred for food. Some groups in the south-east and the south-west also had domestic turkeys; some have suggested that turkeys were domesticated primarily for their feathers.

There is relatively little evidence of large-scale migrations of people over the last several thousand years of North American prehistory, although such migrations did occur. It is fairly well-known, for example, that the

Apache and Navajo probably had a common origin in the subarctic region of western Canada, migrating to the American Southwest between a thousand and several hundred years ago, and relatively quickly adapting their economic, social, and political spheres of culture to fit with their new natural and cultural environments. Another large-scale migration occurred about 1,000 years ago in the Arctic when a group known as the Thule migrated from the west out eastward, replacing populations of Dorset in northern Canada and Greenland. The Thule are ancestral to the contemporary Inuit and Eskimo populations.

HISTORICAL ARCHAEOLOGY

Compared to the amount of archaeological research focused on the prehistoric period, there has been relatively little archaeology done on North American Indigenous peoples during the historic period (i.e., since the arrival of Europeans). There have been some valuable contributions to understanding the impacts of colonialism on Indigenous groups through archaeology in recent years, though, providing a helpful supplement to the oral tradition of Indigenous peoples and the written record. Through excavation, examples have documented the breakdown of traditional cultural patterns following epidemics and other impacts of European colonization; the hybridization of European and Indigenous practices as evidenced through Indigenous symbolism in Christian churches; changes within foodways and material culture; and the ways that some cultural traditions persisted, despite the severity of change brought upon Indigenous peoples and their cultures by Europeans.

Many are surprised to learn that Christopher Columbus was not the first European to discover America. In fact, Columbus never set foot on what is now the continental United States or Canada. John Cabot arrived in what is now eastern Canada in the late 1400s, but the first Europeans arrived 500 years before that. L'Anse aux Meadows is a Norse (or Viking) settlement that dates to approximately AD 1000. It was likely only occupied for a few years, but is representative of a significant presence of Europeans in the north-east part of the continent from several hundred to 1,000 years ago. While their presence at L'Anse aux Meadows did not last long, the Norse did have settlements in Greenland that lasted from about AD 1000 to 1400. There is no consensus regarding why the Norse eventually left what is now Canada and Greenland, but it is commonly thought that they had difficulty adapting to the extreme environments of northern Newfoundland and Greenland and were effectively driven out by the ancestral Indigenous peoples.

FIGURE 3.7

The Expansion of Modern Humans (*Homo sapiens*) around the Globe

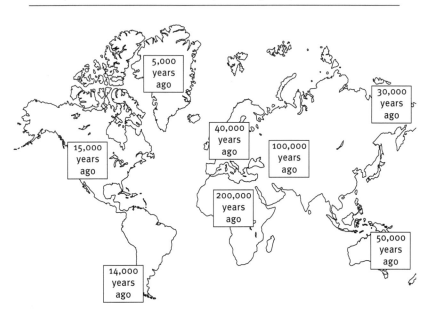

NORTH AMERICAN ARCHAEOLOGY AND PREHISTORY IN A GLOBAL PERSPECTIVE

The Americas were one of the last areas on Earth to be colonized by people. The genus *Homo* has been in Africa for about 2.5 million years; Asia for about 2 million years; and Europe for about 1 million years. *Homo sapiens* have been in Africa for about 200,000 years, Asia for approximately 100,000 years, Australia for 50,000 years, and Western Europe for about 40,000 years.

Most cultural patterns that have been observed in prehistoric North America have been observed elsewhere. One notable exception is the fluted point technology associated with hunting big-game animals. This technique appears to be unique to North America. Many of the cultural patterns observed in North America, particularly in regard to the early prehistoric period of the entire continent and the late prehistoric period of its northern regions, are also found in Asia. Many cultural patterns, especially those in the southern part of the continent, including domestication, are also found in Mesoamerica.

Many of the cultural patterns adopted by North Americans appeared later than they did elsewhere. Communal hunting, the domestication of plants, the rise of more complex social and political structures, the use of pottery, the beginning of art, permanent settlements, the rise of cities, and more all occurred in earlier times outside of North America.

It is important to understand that, although these cultural patterns emerged later in North America than they did elsewhere, this in no way means that the prehistoric inhabitants were not as sophisticated as people elsewhere. None of these cultural patterns are indicative of superior intelligence; nor did they necessarily make life easier.

SUGGESTED READINGS

The website for the National Park Service Archeology Program (www.nps. gov/archeology/sitemap.htm) provides considerable information on the nature of archaeology in the United States. The home page includes links to major sections on archaeology programs, training and education, legislation, reports, and the National Archaeological database.

The premier scholarly journal focusing on North American archaeology and prehistory is *American Antiquity*. The *Canadian Journal of Archaeology* also focuses on the prehistory of Canada. Those interested in the archaeology of Indigenous peoples in historic times are directed to *Across a Great Divide: Continuity and Change in Native North American Societies, 1400–1900*, edited by Laura Scheiber and Mark Mitchell (2010). Some articles on the topic of the archaeology of Indigenous peoples in historic times also occasionally appear in the journal *Historical Archaeology*.

Books that provide good overviews of North American archaeology and prehistory include *Archaeology of Native North America*, by Dean Snow (2010); *Ancient North America: The Archaeology of a Continent*, fourth edition, by Brian Fagan (2005); *A Prehistory of North America*, by Mark Sutton (2011); and *Seeking Our Past: An Introduction to North American Archaeology*, by Sarah Neusius and G. Timothy Gross (2007).

A good book on Indigenous archaeology is *Indigenous Archaeologies: A Reader on Decolonization*, edited by Margaret Bruchac, Siobhan Hart, and M. Martin Wobst (2010).

Alice Beck Kehoe (1998) provides a critical perspective on American archaeology in *The Land of Prehistory: A Critical History of American Archaeology*.

Good overviews of the early period in North American prehistory include *First Peoples in a New World: Colonizing Ice Age America*, by David Meltzer (2009); and *Foragers of the Terminal Pleistocene in North America*, edited by Renne B. Walker and Boyce N. Driskell (2007). The Palaeoindian Database of the Americas provides data on tens of thousands of Palaeoindian artifacts. The website is http://pidba.utk.edu.

Overviews of regional and local prehistories can be found for many parts of the continent in the Smithsonian's *Handbook of North American Indians* series, edited by William Sturtevant.

FOUR

STUDYING POPULATION, LANGUAGES, AND CULTURES IN NORTH AMERICA AS THEY WERE AT AD 1500

INTRODUCTION

This chapter focuses on the methods of reconstructing the populations, languages, and **traditional lifeways** of the Indigenous peoples of North America immediately before the arrival of Europeans in the sixteenth century. Although Europeans had been in the north-east part of the continent before this time, their impact on the populations, languages, and cultures of the Indigenous peoples had been largely insignificant beyond their local areas (i.e., Newfoundland, Greenland). Significant and large-scale impacts on Indigenous peoples and their cultures began with incursions onto the continent by the Spanish in the early 1500s, eventually followed by the English, French, and others.

The objective of much anthropological research on the Indigenous peoples of North America has been to describe what the populations, languages, and cultures were like at approximately AD 1500, before the influence of Europeans was manifested in population loss, language loss, and culture change. These are primarily the cultures that Boas and other anthropologists of the late 1800s and early 1900s were trying to reconstruct.

Regarding population, the chapter provides an overview of the research methods used to reconstruct populations from about AD 1500, and provides some results of that research. Regarding language, the chapter provides an overview of the languages thought to have been spoken around AD 1500, including the number and classification of these languages. The changes in populations and languages that resulted from European incursions are covered in Chapter 6.

TABLE 4.1
Methods Used to Reconstruct Population, Languages, and Traditional
Lifeways

Population
Ecological research (e.g., determining carrying capacity)
Historic research (e.g., considering records of Europeans)
Ethnographic research (e.g., oral history of Indigenous peoples)
Archaeological research (e.g., making inferences from number, size, and structure of
    settlements)

Languages
Historical research (e.g., considering records of Europeans)
Linguistic research (e.g., considering the differences between existing languages)
Ethnographic research (e.g., oral history and contemporary speakers)

Traditional Lifeways
Historical research (e.g., considering the records of Europeans)
Ethnographic research (e.g., oral history and recall ethnography of Indigenous peoples)
Archaeological research (e.g., using sites and artifacts to reconstruct lifeways)

Regarding traditional culture, this chapter covers the fundamental methods and concepts used by anthropologists trying to reconstruct Indigenous
lifeways from approximately AD 1500. It builds upon some of the information on the anthropological perspective covered in Chapter 2. An overview
of traditional lifeways is the focus of Chapter 5.

The principal methods of reconstructing populations, languages, and
traditional lifeways are listed in Table 4.1.

POPULATION AT AD 1500

Estimating the late prehistoric and early historic period populations of
the Indigenous peoples of North America has long been a topic of interest,
extending back into the sixteenth century. The Europeans of the sixteenth
century, subsequent colonial governments, and scholarly researchers
including historians, demographers, and anthropologists have all made
contributions, but there is little consensus on how many people were actually on the continent at AD 1500—or on what the best methods are for
finding this out.

For anthropologists, interest in and research on those early population numbers is considered important for multiple reasons. Population
is integral to understanding all other aspects of culture. Certain kinds of
subsistence strategies, settlement patterns, and social and political institutions, for example, only make sense if populations are within a specific size
range. Thus, when seeking to describe, understand, or explain traditional
cultures, being able to estimate the population size is significant. Know-

ing the numbers of these populations in AD 1500 is also important for being able to chart the impact of Europeans on population loss, in general terms as well as more specifically—for example, through the introduction and spread of disease. Such estimates are important for scholarly reasons, including testing hypotheses about the impacts of colonial processes. They also have an applied anthropological aspect, such as providing data for Indigenous claims about prehistoric use and occupancy of territories.

Population estimates by anthropologists and other scholars have varied widely over the past 100 years. Many early twentieth-century estimates are now considered to have been unrealistically low. Well-known anthropologist Alfred Kroeber, for example, estimated the population at about 1 million. One of the things that many of the early researchers failed to consider was that many populations suffered significant decline through diseases brought by Europeans long before they encountered Europeans themselves, with these diseases spreading through contact between infected and non-infected Indigenous groups.

At the other extreme, some researchers making population estimates in the late twentieth century suggested numbers close to 20 million. Most scholars believe such estimates to be a significant overestimation.

In the early twenty-first century, estimates of the Indigenous population in AD 1500 generally range between 2 and 10 million. Many well-known anthropologists have made estimates. Douglas Ubelaker (2006), for example, suggests there were about 2.4 million; Dean Snow (2010) estimates there were about 3.5 million; Milner and Chaplin (2010) suggest there were about 4 million; and Mark Sutton (2008) suggests 10 million. One of the most well-known scholars focusing on North American Indigenous populations is Indigenous (Cherokee) demographer Russell Thornton (2008), who suggests that the population at about AD 1500 was approximately 7 million.

Variability in population estimates results from the variety of methods used by researchers. There are many different ways to reconstruct populations, and various researchers use different methods, different sets of data, and assign differing weights to variables. The major approaches to estimating population rely on research from ecology, ethnohistory, ethnography, archaeology, and biological anthropology. Most estimates use a combination of different approaches.

Ecological research involves determining the **carrying capacity** of a locality, which requires a reconstruction of the environment before estimating population. Determining the kinds and relative abundance of animals and plants in an area may lead to inferences about how many people could have lived there. The central problem with this approach is that while it allows inferences about how many people the environment could have supported, it does not necessarily prove how many people actually lived there.

Ethnohistoric research on the population at AD 1500 involves examining the written documents detailing these populations, which were created mostly by Europeans; these include letters, journals, and government reports. They often provide valuable information but can have limited use for the many areas of the continent where population loss was significant before the arrival of Europeans in that specific region. Researchers often have to evaluate the records with consideration of the abilities of those doing the recording to compile accurate numbers, especially for groups that were not living in permanent settlements. Some researchers have used the counts of warriors, and from that have estimated village populations based on a fixed number of how many people each warrior represented.

Some researchers have worked with population data for specific Indigenous groups for specific time periods during the historic period to make estimations of the population at AD 1500. Most Indigenous groups in North America reached their lowest population numbers during the 1800s and early 1900s, after which population numbers began to be kept for those specific groups. Researchers calculate the rate of decline over the time the records started being kept and then use the same rate to go back to AD 1500. The problem with this technique is that it is impossible to know whether the rate of decline was steady.

Ethnographic research often takes into account the oral traditions of Indigenous peoples in regard to past populations, but these are of limited value without physical evidence. Often, however, the ethnographic research leads archaeologists to search in specific locations for evidence of villages that were mentioned to ethnographers, which may lead to the kinds of evidence that can be used to estimate populations with increased reliability.

Archaeologists use several different methods for reconstructing population size. The primary method involves making inferences based on habitation dwellings, including the total number of dwellings, size of rooms, and number of rooms. Archaeologists generally use **ethnographic analogy** to support their inferences. For example, if a particular style of Indigenous structure was observed or otherwise known to accommodate 30 people in the historic period, and the same size and shape of structure is observed at a site dating to AD 1500, then those structures are also assumed to have accommodated 30 people.

Archaeologists also use the content and size of refuse deposits (e.g., amount of food refuse, numbers of broken pots, etc.) to make inferences

FIGURE 4.1 Haida Village of Skidegate. A winter village site consisting of several large wooden plank houses, totem and house poles, and canoes on the ocean beach. Photographed by George Dawson, 1878. (Photo courtesy of Royal BC Museum, BC Archives. BCARS B-03360.)

about population size, but these are less reliable conclusions than those using habitation dwellings. Archaeologists recognize that many groups had settlement patterns involving mobility, and so they are careful to account for that in their estimations (e.g., understanding that a group may have had multiple habitation sites within their territory).

Human skeletal remains have limited use in estimating populations. Burial grounds, for example, are rarely found in close proximity to habitation sites, and for mobile groups, burial may have taken place in various areas throughout the territory. Also, many groups preferred to treat their dead in ways other than burial in the ground (e.g., cremation). The analysis of skeletons may lead to data on diet, health, age of death, and the various causes of death, however, which may be factored into population estimates.

Anthropologist Douglas Ubelaker produced estimates of the population of each culture area in North America at the time of initial contact between Indigenous peoples and Europeans (see Table 4.2) by using data on population size included in the regional volumes of the Smithsonian Institution's *Handbook of North American Indians*. The concept of "culture

TABLE 4.2

Population of Indigenous Peoples of North America at Time of Initial Contact with Europeans (based on Ubelaker 2006)

AREA	NUMBER OF PEOPLE	NUMBER/100 SQ KM
Arctic	71,630	3
Subarctic	73,410	1
Northwest Coast	143,600	44
California	216,360	73
Southwest	494,560	31
Great Basin	37,500	4
Plateau	87,000	17
Plains	233,730	8
Northeast	414,930	22
Southeast	586,630	65
TOTAL POPULATION	**2,359,630**	
AVERAGE DENSITY	**14/100 SQ KM**	

area" is elaborated upon in the latter part of this chapter. Readers are cautioned that, although they are based on scholarship, these estimates tend to be quite conservative, falling at the low end of what most anthropologists would accept as the likely range. Despite the conservative bias of the estimates, the table does provide a good comparison to view the differences in population between the various areas of the continent, both in real numbers of people and, no less importantly, in population density.

INDIGENOUS LANGUAGES AT AD 1500

Anthropologists have long been interested in the languages of the Indigenous peoples of North America. Beginning with the first explicitly anthropological research in the 1800s, they have sought to learn, understand, and classify these languages. Almost all anthropologists working firsthand with Indigenous peoples have recognized the value of learning the language of those they seek to study, and many have taken the study of languages as their primary research focus. For some, these languages have been key to communicating with group members and understanding their culture. For others, specific languages became the focus of their studies, with specific interests in sound systems, grammar, vocabulary, and usage. Others have focused on broader or more general issues relating to language, such as the evolution of languages, language comparisons, and classification.

The interest in, and the importance of, the Indigenous languages of North America is expressed by Ives Goddard (1996, 1):

The native languages of North America do not belong to a single family or conform to a single uniform type. For the consideration of general questions in linguistic theory regarding the nature of human languages and its varieties, the North American languages take their places among the languages of the rest of the world. In fact these languages are extraordinarily diverse, and concomitantly they attest some types of linguistic organization that are rare elsewhere and whose study has greatly enriched the understanding of the basic principles of language.

FIGURE 4.2 Frank Bolton Singing. Frank Bolton, also known as Txalaxet or Gitiks, of the Tsmishian Nation in northern British Columbia, recording songs. (Photo by Canadian Museum of Civilization / Marius Barbeau, 1927. Item no. 69595.)

Documenting languages was a primary objective of the anthropologists working with Indigenous groups in the late nineteenth and early twentieth centuries. Boas and others of the time routinely learned the languages of the people they were studying and many attempted to document these languages through writing. Some anthropologists sought to document the languages through sound recordings, as well.

Anthropologists recognize that language is but one kind of communication system exhibited by the Indigenous peoples of North America. Language may be broadly defined as a set of rules governing speech, which in addition to vocabulary include grammar and syntax. Other forms of communication include gestures, signals, rock art, and the creation and use of other kinds of symbols. Although these other kinds of communication often involved creating records, none of these would qualify as a written language.

Considerable anthropological research on languages has focused on identifying the number of distinct languages at AD 1500. A common definition of language is that it is a mutually unintelligible form of speech, which essentially means that two people who do not speak the same language cannot effectively communicate with one another through speech. This differentiates language from dialect; two people speaking different dialects may not understand all the words or language patterns of the other, but they can still effectively communicate.

Attempting to determine the precise number of languages before the arrival of Europeans is problematic, as no Indigenous group of North America had a written form of speech before that time. Consequently, estimates of the number of distinct languages at AD 1500 are largely based on historical records beginning in the 1500s, and the languages that have continued to be spoken since then. Since languages were not written, and there was no technology to record sounds during most of the historic period, estimates also require some speculation, such as distinguishing between dialects and languages.

Despite the problems with estimating the number of languages, it is widely accepted that there were about 400 distinct languages being spoken in North America around AD 1500, and possibly more. About half of those languages continue to exist today. Many are endangered; these languages have very few speakers remaining and their documentation is incomplete.

There is little agreement among anthropological linguists or linguistic anthropologists on how best to classify the Indigenous languages of North America. A simple system includes grouping similar languages into language families. Some examples are included in Table 4.3.

A standard source on the languages of the Indigenous peoples of North America was produced in volume 17 of the *Handbook of North American Indians*, edited by Ives Goddard (1996). In it, Goddard produced what he calls the "Consensus Classification of the Native Languages of North America," placing more than 400 distinct languages into 62 distinct language families.

Placement in the same language family assumes a common origin for the speakers of those now-distinct languages. Linguists, for example, can compare differences in languages and then, using assumptions about the rate of language change, draw inferences about how many hundreds or thousands of years the speakers of the same language have been isolated from each other.

Languages are often used to make, or at least support, inferences about population movements in the past. Being in the same language family as

TABLE 4.3

Languages of the Indigenous Peoples of North America (based on Goddard 1996)*

Language Family	Sample Languages
Eskimo-Aleut	Central Alaskan Yupik, Pacific Yupik, Inupiaq, Western Canadian Inuit, Eastern Canadian Inuit, West Greenlandic, East Greenlandic, Aleut
Algic	Blackfoot, Plains Cree, Woods Cree, Attikamek, Naskapi, Montagnais, Arapaho, Cheyenne, Ojibwa, Algonquian, Ottawa, Kickapoo, Shawnee, Micmac, Yurok, Menominee, Saulteaux, Potawatomi, Abenaki, Mohegan-Pequot, Delaware
Nadene	Tlingit, Eyak, Tahltan, Tanana, Tuchone, Kutchin, Han, Dogrib, Kaska, Sekani, Beaver, Slavey, Chipewyan, Carrier, Chilcotin, Navajo, Western Apache, Eastern Apache, Kiowa Apache
Haida	Haida
Wakashan	Haisla, Heiltsuk, Kwakiutl, Nootka, Makah
Salishan	Bella Coola, Comox, Sechelt, Squamish, Halkomelem, Straits, Clallam, Lushootseed, Twana, Chehalis, Kalispel, Columbian, Lillooet, Thompson, Shuswap, Okanagan, Coeur d'Alene
Tsimshianic	Tsimshian, Nishga, Gitksan
Chinookan	Chinook
Utian	Western Miwok, Eastern Miwok, Northern Costanoan, Southern Costanoan
Yokutsan	Palewyami, Buena Vista, Tule-Kaweah, Gashowu, Valley Yokuts
Plateau Penutian	Klamath, Sahaptin, Nez Perce, Molala
Pomoan	Northeastern Pomo, Southeastern Pomo, Eastern Pomo, Northern Pomo, Central Pomo, Southern Pomo, Kashaya
Yana	Yana
Yukian	Yuki, Wappo
Chumashian	Island Chumash, Obispeno, Purisimeno, Ineseno, Barbareno, Ventureno
Uto-Aztecan	Paiute, Shoshone, Comanche, Ute, Hopi
Kiowa-Tanoan	Kiowa, Jemez, Tiwa, Tewa, Piro
Zuni	Zuni
Siouan-Catawba	Hidatsa, Crow, Mandan, Sioux, Assiniboine, Stoney, Omaha-Ponca, Osage, Chiwere, Winnebago, Biloxi, Catawba
Caddoan	Arikara, Pawnee, Wichita, Caddo
Muskogean	Choctaw, Chickasaw, Appalachee, Alabama, Koasati, Creek, Seminole
Natchez	Natchez
Iroquoian	Huron, Laurentian, Seneca, Cayuga, Mohawk, Oneida, Cherokee
Beothuk	Beothuk

* Note: this table only lists 24 of 62 language families, and a small proportion of over 400 recognized languages. The languages included here are those that non-specialists are most likely to recognize. Those interested in the complete classification are directed to Goddard (1996). The names of some of the languages reflect older spellings or pronunciations in keeping with the standard of the *Handbook of North American Indians*, upon which this table is based.

many languages of the Indigenous groups of western Canada, for example, the languages of the Apache and Navajo support the presumed migrations of those groups from Canada to the American Southwest in the late prehistoric period.

In some cases, languages of various groups are so different that some researchers choose to use much larger distinctions in classification, linking language families into more comprehensive categories such as language phyla. Some researchers propose that the differences between the languages of some groups, even those living in the same regions, are as different from each other as English is to Mandarin or Cantonese. One of the implications is that the substantial differences in languages may reflect multiple migrations to, and within, North America during the prehistoric period.

STUDYING TRADITIONAL LIFEWAYS

In the anthropology of the Indigenous peoples of North America, "traditional lifeways" is usually used to refer to a group's cultural patterns as they existed at AD 1500, or otherwise immediately before the arrival of Europeans. These lifeways include all aspects of culture, including those related to the economic, social, political, and ideological spheres of culture. Although many aspects of Indigenous cultures have changed substantially since the arrival of Europeans, many have not. Many traditional lifeways, especially those related to social and ideological aspects of culture, have persisted through the historic period to contemporary times.

This section outlines the basic methods of reconstructing lifeways as they were immediately before the arrival of Europeans. Chapter 5 provides an overview of the lifeways from that time. Change in lifeways that resulted from the impact of Europeans is covered in Chapter 6, and the persistence of some of the traditional lifeways in contemporary times is included in Chapter 7.

The principal method of anthropological research into traditional lifeways has been **recall ethnography**. Although it was rarely made explicit, it was mostly recall ethnography that Franz Boas and other anthropologists of the late nineteenth and early twentieth centuries were practicing, resulting in the many ethnographies written during that period. The basic technique of recall ethnography consisted of ethnographers working closely with one of more elders or other people in a group who were knowledgeable about that group's life in the past. The people would inform the anthropologist about traditional lifeways based on what they had been told, their own memories, oral history, and personal experience. Potential problems with recall ethnography include faulty memories of informants, informant bias, and deliberate attempts to deceive anthropologists.

FIGURE 4.3 Archaeological Excavation. Excavations often provide key information for reconstructing cultures as they were at AD 1500. (Photo © Barry D. Kass@ImagesofAnthropology.com. Reprinted by permission.)

Many anthropologists using recall ethnography presented the results of their research (i.e., listening to informants) as if the lifeways being described were still being practiced in the present. The ethnographies were written as if they were based on the anthropologists' own observations rather than being recalled by one or more informants; and, as the informants were reflecting on earlier times, they rarely described any kind of European influence. This is often referred to as writing in the **ethnographic present**, which is usually taken to mean describing cultural patterns of the past (i.e., pre-European times in North America) in ways that suggest they are being practiced in the present. Others have described this practice of portraying the Indigenous cultures in the 1800s and 1900s as they were presumed to have existed immediately before the arrival of Europeans as "ethnographic taxidermy."

Other methods of reconstructing lifeways as they were immediately before the arrival of Europeans include oral histories, ethnohistoric documents, and archaeology. Archaeology, in particular, is often used in support of ethnography, oral tradition, and ethnohistory. Archaeologists, for example, can use the archaeological record of sites, artifacts, and ecofacts to not only determine the precise dates of events, but also to reconstruct virtually every aspect of a culture. Basically, the more lines of evidence used in support of an interpretation, the better.

Concept of Culture Area

Culture area is a core concept in anthropology, and is particularly useful for studying the traditional lifeways of the Indigenous cultures of North America. A "culture area" may be defined as a geographic area in which separate societies have similar cultures. Many separate societies, each with its own distinctive culture, exist in a single culture area. Despite there being many cultural distinctions between the groups of any particular area, when taken as a whole, the lifeways of all those within a single culture area contrast with the lifeways of Indigenous groups in other culture areas.

The use of the "culture area" concept is not without controversy. The term has a long history in North American anthropology, with the basic concept originating in the late 1800s and being further developed and gaining wide use in the early 1900s. It remains in wide use in studies with a focus on traditional lifeways.

Advocates of the concept, past and present, suggest that it is an excellent heuristic device, allowing researchers to put order into considerable cultural diversity around the continent, which in turn enables them to compare and understand cultures. In this regard the concept is particularly useful when focusing on ecological adaptations, and it works well for those who see cultures as primarily an adaptation to the environment.

Those who criticize the use of the concept tend to focus on the problems occurring with the oversimplification of complex phenomena (i.e., cultures), and recognize that while "culture area" is useful for providing generalizations, it remains an arbitrary, artificial construct that fails to adequately consider a number of factors, including the diversity of cultures within regions; the way environments change; the way cultures change; the many cases where a group may exhibit a combination of traits characteristic of different culture areas; and many other exceptions. Critics also point out the problem of lack of a consensus on how to define the distinguishing natural and cultural characteristics of culture areas. Thus, the defining characteristics of a culture area may change from researcher to researcher.

Despite criticism of the concept, most contemporary anthropologists interested in the traditional lifeways of North American Indigenous peoples continue to use "culture area," although they recognize its limitations. There is no universal agreement on the number or defining characteristics of each culture area, but most recognize that there are ten areas, as illustrated in Figure 4.4. Well-known Indigenous groups of each area are listed

FIGURE 4.4
Culture Areas of North America

TABLE 4.4

Major Indigenous Groups, by Culture Area*

ARCTIC	Aleut, Eskimo, Inuit
SUBARCTIC	Beothuk, Chipewyan, Cree, Dene (Athapaskan), Dogrib, Kaska, Innu, Micmac, Northern Algonkians
NORTHWEST COAST	Bella Coola (Nuxalk), Chinook, Coast Salish, Eyak, Haida, Kwakiutl (Kwakwaka'wakw), Makah, Nisga'a, Nootka (Nuu-chah-nulth), Tlingit, Tsmishian, Yurok
PLATEAU	Coeur d'Alene, Interior Salish (Shuswap, Lillooet, Thompson, Okanagan), Nez Perce, Spokane, Yakama
GREAT BASIN	Bannock, Paiute, Shoshoni, Ute, Washo
CALIFORNIA	Chumash, Miwok, Modoc, Ohlone, Patwin, Pomo, Salinan, Wintun, Yahi, Yana, Yokut, Yorok
PLAINS	Arapaho, Blackfoot, Blood, Cheyenne, Comanche, Crow, Dakota, Lakota, Hidatsa, Iowa, Kiowa, Mandan, Osage, Pawnee, Piegan, Sioux, Wichita
SOUTHWEST	Acoma, Apache, Hopi, Navajo, Pima, Tohono O'Odham, Zuni
SOUTHEAST	Alabama, Caddo, Catawa, Cherokee, Chickasaw, Choctaw, Creek, Natchez, Seminole
NORTHEAST	Algonquin, Cayuga, Chippewa, Erie, Ojibwa, Delaware, Huron, Illinois, Iroquois, Kickapoo, Mahican, Menominee, Miami, Micmac, Mohawk, Oneida, Onondaga, Ottawa, Pequot, Seneca, Shawnee, Winnebago, Wyandot

* Note: this is a generalized overview of the major well-known Indigenous groups of each culture area at approximately AD 1500. It is not comprehensive, and many groups are not listed. Since there is no consensus on the boundaries of culture areas, and since some groups had traditional territory in more than one area, groups may be listed in more than one area. Mostly, the historic names of groups are used. The list includes alternate names or subgroups of larger ethnic groups (e.g., the Dakota as a subgroup of the Sioux).

in Table 4.4 and the physical characteristics of each area are described in the following paragraphs.

Arctic: The Arctic is the northernmost culture area of North America, incorporating northern Alaska, much of Northern Canada, and Greenland. It runs east-west across the entire continent and is bordered on the south by the Subarctic. It is characterized by long, cold winters and short, mild summers, with little plant life that is useful as food for humans, moderate amounts of game animals in some areas, and considerable sea mammals. The northern parts of the Arctic have limited land resources but the southern portion includes tundra, providing a suitable habitat for caribou and other game animals. Natural resources include plentiful sea mammals off the coasts and islands; and caribou and other game animals in the southern inland areas.

Subarctic: Lying south of the Arctic, the Subarctic encompasses much of the rest of Canada. It is bordered by the Northwest Coast, Plateau, Plains, and Northeast culture areas. The physical environment is characterized by boreal forest, tundra, cold winters, and mild summers. Natural resources include moose, caribou, deer, and other game animals, and a diverse array of vegetation useful for food and shelter.

Northwest Coast: The Northwest Coast comprises a relatively thin strip on the Pacific Coast, beginning in Alaska and extending south along the coasts of British Columbia, Washington, and Oregon to northern California. The area is physically characterized by a rugged, mountainous coastline, a mild and wet climate, and plentiful natural resources, especially salmon and cedar. To the north it is bordered by the Subarctic. To the east lies the Subarctic and Plateau culture areas, and to the south is the California culture area. Plants and animals are extremely diverse and abundant.

California: California exhibits perhaps the greatest environmental diversity of all of these culture areas. The area extends southward from the northern part of the state, west of the Sierras. It is bordered by the Northwest Coast, Great Basin, and Southwest culture areas. Natural resources include a tremendous variety of foods, including both maritime and terrestrial mammals, and a wide diversity of plant foods such as acorns and berries.

Plateau: The Plateau includes the southern interior of British Columbia, as well as parts of Washington, Oregon, Montana, and Idaho. It is drained by the Fraser and Columbia rivers, both of which contain abundant salmon on annual migrations. It is bordered by the Subarctic, the Plains, the Great Basin, and the Northwest Coast. There are abundant varieties of edible plants and animals.

Great Basin: The Great Basin includes Nevada, Utah, and portions of Washington, Oregon, Idaho, Wyoming, and Colorado. It is characterized as a large, arid environment consisting of mountain ranges and more than 100 basins. Natural resources are few, producing a relatively low carrying capacity for human populations.

Southwest: The Southwest includes all or portions of the south-west American states, including Arizona, New Mexico, the southern portions of Colorado and Utah, a small portion of south-east California, and northern Mexico. It is bordered by Mesoamerica to the south, the Plains and Great Basin to the north, and California to the west. The area includes tributaries of the Colorado and Rio Grande rivers. A variety of environmental zones exist in the Southwest, but it is generally characterized by a hot and dry climate, which includes deserts. Although the area is dry, plants and animals are still plentiful.

Plains: The Plains includes the southern parts of the Canadian Prairie Provinces of Alberta, Saskatchewan, and Manitoba, and extends south from Minnesota and the Dakotas through the central states to Texas and the Gulf of Mexico. East to west, it extends from the Mississippi Valley to the Rocky Mountains. It is bordered by the Subarctic, Plateau, Great Basin, Southwest, Southeast, and Northeast. It is physically characterized by a relatively flat landscape covered mostly with grasslands. Natural resources include buffalo.

Northeast: The Northeast includes the north-east American states and the south-east part of Canada, including the Great Lakes area. It extends from southern Ontario to the Canadian Maritime provinces (Nova Scotia, New Brunswick, and Prince Edward Island). In the US it extends eastward from Ohio to the New England states. It is bordered by the Subarctic, Plains, and Southeast culture areas. The environment was mostly forested in prehistoric times, with cold winters and warm summers.

Southeast: The Southeast culture area includes the south-eastern American states, extending from Illinois east to Virginia, south to Florida, and west to Louisiana and eastern Texas. It is bordered by the Plains and Northeast culture areas. The area was naturally forested in prehistoric times, but many groups kept parts of it cleared to facilitate farming and easier hunting. The environment also included marshes and everglades.

MAJOR AREAS OF INTEREST IN THE STUDY OF TRADITIONAL LIFEWAYS AT AD 1500

The ethnographers of the late nineteenth and early twentieth centuries usually attempted to address each of the major aspects of traditional lifeways, at least as they were considered at that time. There was no template used by these ethnographers, but in general the focus was on subsistence strategy, diet, settlement patterns, housing, social systems, political systems, and ideology (see Table 4.5). Lesser attention was devoted to technology, material culture, arts, and exchange within and between groups. Following are the basic concepts and terminology used by anthropologists in describing these aspects of culture.

Subsistence strategy refers to the way people get their food. Major strategies being used by Indigenous people at AD 1500 included **generalized foraging**, **specialized** (or complex) **foraging**, and **horticulture**. Early ethnographers usually described how people got their food, but these descriptions were often not very detailed and did not use the terminology that is in use today.

Diet refers to the specific foods that people ate. Describing the diet of people before the arrival of Europeans was a standard feature of early ethnographies, and was often very detailed.

TABLE 4.5
Major Areas of Anthropological Interest in the Study of Traditional
Lifeways

Subsistence Strategy
Focusing on how people get their food.

Diet
Focusing on what plants and animals they were eating.

Settlement Patterns
Focusing on how sites were distributed across the landscape and when they were used.

Housing
Focusing on the structure and function of houses.

Social Systems
Focusing on marriage and family patterns, and on ways of tracing descent, kinship, and
social inequality.

Political Systems
Focusing on how groups were organized, such as bands, tribes, or chiefdoms.

Ideology
Focusing on belief systems, mythology, shamanism, ritual, values, and world view.

The Arts
Focusing on both the visual and performing arts.

Technology
Focusing on how people made things like artifacts and houses, as well as how they did
things like hunting and cooking.

Settlement patterns has various meanings, ranging from the general distribution of sites on the landscape to the use of traditional territories, to the layout of specific settlements. Common patterns at AD 1500 included highly mobile (or nomadic); semi-sedentary; and sedentary. Early ethnographies typically included descriptions of how people used their landscapes, including general movements through their territories at various times of the year.

Housing refers to the habitation structures of people. Most early ethnographies provide descriptions of the structures commonly in use before the arrival of Europeans.

Social systems, also known as social strategies, social organization, and social institutions, refers to the way people relate to each other. The term includes aspects of kinship, descent, marriage and family patterns, social stratification, and ways of maintaining social control. Many early ethnographies devoted considerable amounts of description to social systems, including the various kinds of kinship and descent groups (e.g., **lineages** and **clans**), ways of tracing descent (e.g., **matrilineal** or **patrilineal**), and patterns of social stratification (e.g., **egalitarian** or **stratified**).

Political systems, also known as political strategies, political organization, and political institutions, refers to the way people maintain order within and between groups. Common types of political systems in North America at AD 1500 included bands, tribes, and **chiefdoms**. Political systems were typically described in early ethnographies.

Ideology refers to beliefs and values. Principal components of ideology include mythology, shamanism, and ritual. Most early ethnographies included substantial description of ideology, including the documentation of many myths.

Arts refers to both the visual and performing arts. Visual arts include painting, carving, sculpture, and design elements. The art may be stand-alone, such as rock art and totem poles, or it may be incorporated as design elements in pottery, baskets, and other artifacts and habitation structures. Performing arts include dance, music, and song. All Indigenous groups had art in AD 1500. Many early ethnographers included descriptions of art, but it was usually a minor part of their ethnographies.

Technology refers to the way people make things, such as how they make their tools and houses. Early ethnographies usually paid relatively little attention to technology. When it was described it often focused solely on the building of houses.

STUDYING POPULATION, LANGUAGES, AND TRADITIONAL LIFEWAYS IN A GLOBAL PERSPECTIVE

The interests of anthropologists and others in studying population, languages, and traditional lifeways of Indigenous peoples at AD 1500 are shared around the world by those interested in Indigenous peoples without written records, and especially by those researchers focusing on the impacts of European incursions and colonialism.

The methods used by anthropologists and others in attempting to reconstruct late prehistoric and early historic period populations of Indigenous peoples are no different in North America than they are elsewhere. Similarly, issues related to determining the number and classification of languages are common elsewhere.

The concept of "culture area" as it is used by North American anthropologists is rare outside of North America. Its use remains primarily restricted to studies of the Indigenous peoples and cultures of North America in late prehistoric and early historic times. Anthropologists elsewhere recognize and use broad categories, such as "North America" and "Mesoamerica," to recognize the broad and comprehensive distinctions that characterize regions on very large scales, but the degree to which the concept of culture area is used in North America is not common elsewhere.

SUGGESTED READINGS

The Smithsonian Institution's *Handbook of North American Indians*, under the general editorship of William Sturtevant, is an excellent source. *Volume 3: Environment, Origins, and Populations*, edited by Douglas Ubelaker (2006), includes multiple contributions on populations. *Volume 17: Languages*, edited by Ives Goddard (1996), is devoted entirely to Indigenous languages of North America.

FIVE

OVERVIEW OF TRADITIONAL LIFEWAYS

INTRODUCTION

This chapter provides a broad overview of traditional lifeways as they were immediately before the arrival of Europeans. The information is based primarily on ethnographic, historical, and archaeological studies.

SUBSISTENCE STRATEGIES AND DIET

The Indigenous peoples of North America exhibited diverse subsistence strategies, incorporating a wide variety of foods; both plants and animals, wild and domestic. The strategies of generalized foraging, specialized foraging, and horticulture were all evident before the arrival of Europeans. Some groups only exhibited generalized foraging, while others exhibited a combination of strategies.

Providing overviews of subsistence strategies and diet is somewhat problematic, since not all food resources were available to all groups in any one given culture area. The information presented here is very generalized. It was not unusual for specific groups to incorporate dozens of animal species and more than 100 varieties of plants into their diet. Overall, more than 1,500 species of plants have been identified as being used as foods by the Indigenous peoples of North America (see Box 5.1).

Peoples of the Arctic were generalized foragers. They depended primarily on maritime resources, especially seals, but also other sea mammals such as sea lions and walrus. Whales were both hunted and scavenged. Sea-mammal hunting occurred in kayaks, in larger open boats, and through holes drilled in ice, and usually with the use of harpoons. Other important maritime resources included fish and sea birds. Terrestrial animals such as

---

BOX 5.1

Ethnobotany of the Indigenous Peoples of North America

Ethnobotanist Daniel Moerman has spent more than two decades researching the use of plants by the Indigenous peoples of North America. His research has included studying both anthropological and historical sources, and he has produced three comprehensive books on the ethnobotany of the Indigenous Peoples of North America (Moerman 1998; 2009; 2010).

Moerman has identified 47,000 uses of 3,860 species of plants. This includes more than 1,500 species used for food and more than 2,500 used as medicines. Plants were also used for dyes, weaving, and construction.

Plants with the greatest number of uses as food include chokecherry (*Prunus virginiana*), banana yucca (*Yucca baccata*), corn (*Zea mays*), Saskatoon serviceberry (*Amelanchier alnifolia*), honey mesquite (*Posopis glandulosa*), American red raspberry (*Rubis idaeus*), saguaro (*Carnegia gigantea*), salmonberry (*Rubus spectabilis*), thimbleberry (*Rubus parviflorus*), and broadleaf cattail (*Typha latifolia*).

Ethnobotanists recognize distinct categories of food plants for the Indigenous peoples of North America. Major categories include appetizer; baby food; beverage; bread and cake; candy; dessert; dietary aid (e.g., making food more digestible; providing a source of vitamins); fruit; porridge (a thick liquid made by boiling grains or legumes); preservative; sauce and relishes; soup; spice; sweetener; and vegetable.

Plants with the greatest number of uses as medicine include common yarrow (*Achillia millefolium*), calamus (*Acorus calamus*), big sagebrush (*Artemisia tridentate*), fernleaf biscuitroot (*Lomatium dissectum*), common chokecherry (*Prunus virginiana*), Louisiana sagewort (*Artemisia ludoviciana*), devil's club (*Oplopanax horridus*), common juniper (*Juniperus communis*), Canadian mint (*Mentha canadensis*), and stinging nettle (*Urtica dioica*).

Major categories of medicinal use include abortifacient (inducing abortion); analgesic (pain relief); anesthetic (reducing one's sense of touch or pain); antidiarrheal (stopping diarrhea); antidote (negating effects of poison); burn dressings; carminative (relieving flatulence/gas); cold remedy; contraceptive; diuretic (causing urination); hallucinogen; hemorrhoid remedy; laxative; narcotic; sedative; stimulant; toothache remedy; and vertigo remedy (dizziness).

---

bears, moose, musk ox, and caribou were important for groups living in areas where those animals resided. Few plants were available to the Indigenous peoples of the Arctic.

Like the peoples of the Arctic, Subarctic groups were also generalized foragers, but they had less dependence on maritime resources and more on terrestrial plants and animals of the boreal forest. Key food animals included caribou, elk, moose, and deer. Those on the east coast also hunted sea mammals. Many groups fished, and smaller animals such as ducks, hares, muskrats, beavers, and gophers were hunted or trapped. Where available, people hunted mountain goats and mountain sheep. Plant foods included a diversity of wild berries, root crops, and mushrooms. Many groups created **pemmican**, a mixture of meat, fat, and berries that could last for months.

Groups of the Northwest Coast may be characterized as specialized (or complex) foragers. They had an extremely diverse diet of marine and ter-

TABLE 5.1

Subsistence Strategies of the Indigenous Peoples of North America, by Culture Area

	Principal Strategies	Key Resources
ARCTIC	generalized foraging	sea mammals
SUBARCTIC	generalized foraging	large game animals
NORTHWEST COAST	specialized foraging	salmon
PLATEAU	specialized foraging	salmon
GREAT BASIN	generalized foraging	pinyon nuts
CALIFORNIA	generalized and specialized foraging	acorns
PLAINS	foraging and horticulture	buffalo
SOUTHWEST	horticulture and generalized foraging	corn, beans, squash
NORTHEAST	horticulture and generalized foraging	corn and beans
SOUTHEAST	horticulture and generalized foraging	corn, beans, squash

Note: the key resources are highly simplified. Most groups incorporated hundreds of varieties of plants and animals into their diets.

restrial resources, focusing on salmon. Using nets and spears, they often worked cooperatively in large groups to harvest the fish that were on their way to spawn upstream in rivers; and they also cooperated to preserve the fish by drying and smoking them. People were able to harvest enough salmon in a few weeks in late summer and early autumn for it to last as a primary staple through the winter months. Diets were supplemented with a wide variety of other foods including waterfowl, shellfish, sea mammals, deer, many other kinds of fish and terrestrial animals, and more than 100 varieties of plants.

Like those on the Northwest Coast, groups on the Plateau may also be described as specialized foragers due to their focus on salmon. They did not have access to sea mammals and other coastal resources, but they incorporated many other kinds of plants and animals into their diet. Key terrestrial animals included deer and elk, although rabbits, squirrels, and other small animals were often used as well. More than 100 plants are known to have been used for food by Plateau groups.

Plains groups exhibited aspects of both foraging and horticulture. The key resource for many was buffalo (bison), which were usually obtained through communal hunting practices such as driving them off cliffs or to other places where they became vulnerable. (Buffalo hunting was done on

FIGURE 5.1 Cutting up a Whale. Three women in Alaska cutting up a beluga whale. Whale meat is shown drying on racks in the background. (Photo by Edward S. Curtis. Courtesy of the Library of Congress.)

foot. Horses were not native to North America; they were first incorporated into buffalo hunting in the late 1500s when they were obtained from the Spanish.) Prior to the arrival of Europeans, many peoples of the Plains were farmers, settling in the large river valleys. Even those who farmed depended on buffalo and other animals, however. Besides buffalo, other animals used for food included deer, elk, antelope, rabbits, wild turkeys, waterfowl, and fish. Wild plants used as food included varieties of roots and fruits. Like those in the Subarctic, people of the Plains were able to preserve meat in the form of pemmican.

Peoples of the Great Basin were primarily foragers, although some groups incorporated horticulture into their diets. For many, the key resource was the wild pinyon nut, which provided an excellent source of Nutrition, was easily stored, and could be ground into flour. They also relied on other kinds of plants such as grasses, acorns, root crops, nuts, berries, and beans. Animals used for food included waterfowl, deer, sheep, bison, elk, rabbits, reptiles, insects, and fish.

FIGURE 5.2 Berry Gatherers. Mandan women, from the Plains culture area, gathering berries. (Photo by Edward S. Curtis. Courtesy of the Library of Congress.)

California groups were primarily foragers, exploiting plentiful resources in diverse environments. For many the key resource was acorns, which were easily stored, provided excellent nutrition, and could be processed in a variety of ways, including making them into bread or a form of mush. Other important plant foods included a diversity of Nuts, grasses, roots, and berries. Animals used for food included deer, elk, antelope, and smaller animals such as rabbits, rodents, and insects. Fish were also an important part of the California diet, and those along the coastal areas often focused on hunting sea mammals, such as seals and sea lions, and on collecting shellfish.

Northeast groups exhibited diverse subsistence strategies. Some groups in the north-east part of the area maintained a generalized foraging adaptation, hunting both sea and land mammals, fishing, collecting shellfish, and gathering plants. Most groups, however, maintained subsistence through a combination of foraging and horticulture. Key horticultural crops included corn and beans. Wild animals used for food included deer, elk, and many smaller mammals. Birds, such as ducks, geese, grouse, and turkeys were also part of the diet. Fish were an important resource, and where available, buffalo were also hunted. Important wild plants included varieties of fruits and nuts.

In the Southeast, subsistence was based primarily on horticulture. The most important crops for farming were corn, beans, and squash. Wild plants incorporated in the diet included a diversity of nuts, seeds, vegetables, berries, and fruits. Animals used for food included fish, deer, bears, other smaller mammals, rodents, rabbits, reptiles, turkeys, waterfowl, insects, and shellfish.

In the Southwest, subsistence for some groups was primarily based on horticulture, while for others it was primarily based on foraging. Most groups practiced both, but to varying degrees. The dominant domestic crops, as in the Southeast and Mesoamerica, were corn, beans, and squash. Wild plant foods incorporated into the Southwest diet included varieties of cacti, nuts, grasses, seeds, and berries. Animals used as food included fish, turkeys, deer, antelope, mountain sheep, rabbits, other small mammals, waterfowl, and insects.

Overall, in general terms, horticulture was a dominant subsistence strategy in the Southwest, Southeast, and Northeast. It was also practiced in parts of the Plains and Great Basin, though it was not as dominant there. Foraging was evident throughout the continent. Specialized (or complex) foraging was evident in the Northwest Coast and Plateau regions, focusing on salmon; on the Plains, focusing on buffalo; and in California, focusing on acorns. Generalized foraging was the norm elsewhere and was the primary strategy in the Arctic, Subarctic, and Great Basin.

The Indigenous peoples of North America are not known for incorporating domestic animals into their diets, although there is evidence that domestic animals were kept. Domestic dogs have a long history in North America and many believe that they may have accompanied the first migrants to the continent over 14,000 years ago. They were probably kept primarily to assist in hunting, as protectors, and as pets rather than for food. In the case of the Arctic peoples, dogs were also used to pull sleds. There is also evidence of domestic turkeys being kept both in the Southeast and the Southwest. They likely played a minor part in the subsistence base of these groups, and some have suggested the primary reason for domestication may have been their feathers rather than their meat.

Settlement Patterns and Housing

There is a strong correlation between subsistence strategies and settlement patterns. Typically, those who were generalized foragers tended to exhibit high mobility; specialized foragers tended to be semi-sedentary; and those who practiced horticulture were sedentary. Common settlement patterns and housing for each culture are identified in Table 5.2.

Although generalized foragers were the most mobile, they still typically maintained a traditional territory. Movement was primarily associated with the harvesting of seasonal resources. While each group maintained a core territory, the peripheral areas were often shared with neighboring groups. One group may have used a particular area for harvesting some kind of plant in the spring, for example, while another group may have used the same area for hunting in the fall. Neighboring groups would occasionally come together to harvest particular resources cooperatively (e.g., hunting herd animals, fishing salmon, gathering nuts) and to socialize.

Since specialized foragers were usually able to harvest and process enough of a particular kind of food to create a substantial surplus, they tended to be less mobile. In the Northwest Coast and Plateau culture areas, for example, groups would congregate to harvest and process salmon, creating enough of a surplus to last them through the winter. Winter villages could then be occupied for at least four or five months, and returned to annually (e.g., the Haida village of Skidegate was a Northwest Coast winter village; See Figure 4.1).

Horticulture correlates with sedentism. Farming tends to produce enough food to both allow and require people to create permanent settlements. The amount of food surplus created by farming decreases the need for extended hunting and gathering excursions. Although horticulturalists typically supplemented their diets through hunting animals and gathering wild plants, they were usually able to make these forays less frequently than other groups did; and they would have been able to spend all or most of the year at a single settlement. Also, effective horticulture requires constant labor, including preparing fields, as well as protecting, tending, harvesting, and processing crops.

There was considerable variability in the kinds of habitation structures in North America before the arrival of Europeans. See, for example, Figures 1.4 (Taos Pueblo), 2.4 (King Island village), 4.1 (Skidegate), and 5.3 (Plains tipis). Typically, the effort put into building a structure was a reflection of how long the people planned on being there, and the kinds of building resources that were available to them. **Igloos** and small structures constructed of pole or branch frameworks covered with vegetation, for

TABLE 5.2
Settlement Patterns and Housing, by Culture Area

	Typical Settlement Pattern	Typical Housing
ARCTIC	mobile	igloos, skin tents, pithouses
SUBARCTIC	mobile	pole frames with skin or vegetation
PLATEAU	semi-sedentary	winter pithouse villages
NORTHWEST COAST	semi-sedentary	winter plankhouse villages
PLAINS	mobile	tipis
GREAT BASIN	mobile	wikiups
CALIFORNIA	mobile, semi-sedentary	mostly pole frames covered with vegetation
SOUTHWEST	semi-sedentary, sedentary	pueblos, hogans, wikiups
NORTHEAST	semi-sedentary, sedentary	longhouses, wigwams
SOUTHEAST	sedentary	permanent villages and houses

example, could often be constructed by a few people in less than an hour. This kind of structure was therefore ideal for highly mobile groups.

Housing also often reflects climate, both in the kinds of material people had to work with and the conditions they had to adapt to. Peoples in areas of few trees, brush, or reeds, for example, had to look to other sources for shelter, such as stone, animal skins, adobe, or earth. Many groups in North America constructed semi-subterranean structures consisting of a dug-out depression overlaid with a log framework and covered with earth. This kind of structure was very effective for insulating against the cold and was widely used in cold environments. Semi-subterranean houses are often known as **pithouses**.

Generalized foragers, knowing they were only going to be in an area for a short time, often built temporary shelters that would be used only once. If they knew they were going to be returning for extended periods on an annual basis, then they may have put more effort into the building so that it could be used repeatedly.

Arctic peoples tended to be quite mobile and had a few different kinds of shelters. For temporary winter shelters, they would often build igloos. In some cases they would build tent-like structures covered with animal skins. Some groups occasionally built large, semi-subterranean houses, with frameworks made from driftwood and whalebones and then covered with earth.

Subarctic groups generally created temporary shelters from a framework of poles that was covered with vegetation or animal skins. Some built semi-subterranean houses, with a framework of logs covered with earth, for winter use.

In the Plateau, people usually lived in villages consisting of several semi-subterranean houses in the winter months, with each house holding a few dozen people or more. During other times of the year people traveled in smaller groups and lived in temporary structures created with a pole framework that was covered with vegetation or animal skins.

Northwest Coast people lived in villages comprised of several large houses constructed of cedar, often known as plankhouses (see Figure 4.1), during the winter months. Each structure housed multiple families, usually comprising at least a few dozen and sometimes over 100 people. They would use logs for the framework and then create planks for the walls and roofs. For the remainder of the year they would travel in smaller groups, usually building temporary shelters using local vegetation. Some groups would dismantle the cedar planks from the winter houses and transport them, attached to the sides of their canoes, for use in their spring, summer, and autumn shelters.

The peoples of the Plains usually lived in tipis (or teepees), which were created from a conical arrangement of poles overlaid with animal skins. Those who were involved in farming tended to live in villages of large, earth-covered shelters with log frameworks near the fields, but when they were away from the horticultural villages they would use tipis. Those who were primarily dependent on foraging usually took the tipi components with them when moving locations.

Housing in the Great Basin was variable. A common kind of shelter was known as a wikiup (a dome-shaped structure constructed from poles and brush). Some groups also lived in semi-subterranean houses during the winter.

The California culture area exhibited a variety of housing styles, reflecting the diversity of its environments. Northern California groups sometimes built plankhouses similar to those of the Northwest Coast. There were some semi-subterranean houses, but most housing was created using a branch framework over which some kind of vegetation was placed. One common type included oval-shaped or circular structures with a branch framework that was covered with tule mats or grasses. As with groups in other culture areas, peoples in California would live in different kinds of shelters at different times of the year.

In the Southwest, two kinds of houses were common. Settled farmers living in pueblos, such as the Hopi and Zuni, lived in houses built with adobe, or wood and stone coated with a mud plaster. Often the houses

FIGURE 5.3 Plains Tipi Village, 1908. (Photo by Edward S. Curtis. Courtesy of the Library of Congress.)

were built like apartments, with multiple levels and interconnected rooms. The non-pueblo peoples, such as the Navajo and Apache, lived in wikiups or **hogans**.

In the Northeast, many people spent most or all of the year in large, multi-family structures known as **longhouses**, which could be more than 100 feet long. The houses were usually built with logs, saplings, and bark. Longhouse villages were often surrounded with palisades. When away from the longhouse villages, groups would often reside in small, temporary, tipi-like structures covered with animal skins or vegetation. One variety, called a wigwam, was made up of a pole framework with a covering of mats or birch bark.

Groups in the Southeast tended to live in permanent villages. Villages were often surrounded with palisades, and houses of important people were often built on top of earthen mounds. It was common for people to have two homes in close proximity, and these were commonly described as their winter houses and summer houses. Houses were often constructed with cane withes and clay, topped with thatched roofs, and some were covered with dried mud for insulation. Summer houses were often built on raised posts for better ventilation during the warmer months.

SOCIAL SYSTEMS

Social systems varied widely among Indigenous groups. There were also strong correlations between social systems and other aspects of culture, such as subsistence. For example, generalized foragers tended to have the simplest and most egalitarian social systems. The systems of specialized foragers and horticulturalists tended to be increasingly complex. The most important social unit for each group, according to culture area, is listed in Table 5.3.

In the Arctic, the **nuclear family** was the most important social and economic grouping, although the **extended family** was also important and often lived together. Kinship was recognized beyond the nuclear and extended families, but kinship groups and descent groups were not very important.

In the Subarctic, like the Arctic, the nuclear and extended families were also the primary social and economic units, with bands generally being egalitarian. Kinship and descent groups were important among some groups, but they carried few rights and responsibilities. Descent was traced bilaterally. Some groups recognized membership in specific clans.

Among Plateau groups, extended families and lineages were important, with membership in specific lineages dictating rights and responsibilities. Stratification was common but flexible.

On the Northwest Coast, the major social and economic unit was the **house**—a group of extended families living in the same house during the winter months. The house operated like a corporation, and in today's studies it is sometimes referred to as a corporate group. Membership in houses and larger clans was important, carrying rights and responsibilities. Northern groups generally traced descent matrilineally, while southern groups traced descent either patrilineally or bilaterally. Groups in the northern Northwest Coast usually exhibited a ranking system while the southern groups exhibited more of a class system.

Like groups in the Arctic and Subarctic, the people of the Great Basin groups had their nuclear and extended families as the basic social and economic units within the generally egalitarian structure of their bands. Kinship and descent groups were not important.

In California, social systems were variable. In areas with a rich resource base, groups often exhibited a complex social structure, with lineages being a primary social unit and clans and class structure being common. In areas with fewer resources, groups tended to be more egalitarian, with nuclear or extended families functioning as the primary social units.

In the Southwest, social systems varied. Among some groups, nuclear and extended families were of primary importance; in other groups, lineages were key. Some groups traced descent matrilineally and other groups traced it bilaterally.

TABLE 5.3
Important Social and Economic Units, by Culture Area

	Most Important Social and Economic Units
ARCTIC	nuclear and extended families
SUBARCTIC	nuclear and extended families
PLATEAU	extended families and lineages
NORTHWEST COAST	houses and clans
PLAINS	extended families and sodalities
GREAT BASIN	nuclear and extended families
CALIFORNIA	extended families and lineages
SOUTHWEST	extended families and lineages
NORTHEAST	lineages and clans
SOUTHEAST	lineages and clans

In the Plains, extended families were important social and economic units. **Sodalities** (non-kin-based associations, such as warrior societies) were also important social units, particularly for maintaining alliances.

Among both the Northeast and Southeast groups, lineages and clans were important, especially for those based on horticulture. It was the lineage that tended to determine who would govern the fields. Descent in both areas was usually traced matrilineally.

POLITICAL SYSTEMS

The political systems of the Indigenous peoples of North America before the arrival of Europeans are often categorized as bands, tribes, or chiefdoms.

Bands may be generally characterized as having less than 50 people; high mobility; an egalitarian social structure; informal leadership; and a generalized forager subsistence strategy. Bands are autonomous, independent groups that make their decisions independently of other groups. Usually, all bands in a region are consistently either male or female exogamous, meaning that all or most of the adult males or adult females have married into the bands. Consequently, band members usually have relatives in many nearby bands. Bands tend to maintain strong social and economic alliances with neighboring groups, but act independently. They usually consist of a group of related families, but membership is fluid.

Tribes are also known as segmentary societies. They typically have a population ranging from a few hundred to a few thousand, scattered among multiple settlements. Subsistence is often based on horticulture or

TABLE 5.4
Political Systems, by Culture Area

	Common Political System
ARCTIC	band-like
SUBARCTIC	band-like
PLATEAU	tribe-like
NORTHWEST COAST	chiefdom-like
PLAINS	tribe-like
GREAT BASIN	band-like
CALIFORNIA	tribe-like, chiefdom-like
SOUTHWEST	tribe-like, chiefdom-like
NORTHEAST	tribe-like, confederacies
SOUTHEAST	chiefdom-like

the ability of foragers to effectively create substantial surplus from wild plants and animals. Villages often have a local leader, but leadership is often informal, or it may be characteristic of the beginnings of formal leadership. Anthropologists often call such a leader a headman or bigman. The leader often has influence but no real authority within or beyond the local village. There is no overarching authority or leader of all the villages comprising a tribe. Sodalities, also known as pan-tribal associations, are an important mechanism for maintaining alliances between villages.

Chiefdoms usually number from a few thousand to tens of thousands of people. Subsistence is usually based on horticulture or the ability of specialized foragers to create substantial surplus in resource-rich areas. Chiefdoms exhibit significant social inequality, social classes, and formal leadership that is determined through heredity.

There are close correlations between political systems and other aspects of culture, such as subsistence, settlement patterns, and social systems. Table 5.4 lists the typical forms of political organization by culture area.

Arctic, Subarctic, and Great Basin groups were generally organized as bands. Plains groups are generally considered to have been organized as tribes.

It is difficult to categorize the Plateau groups into any of the major categories, as they exhibited features of each. People would live and travel in small, band-like groups for much of the year, but then come together to live in larger units during the winter. They also exhibited signs of tribes and chiefdoms in regards to the importance of lineages to economic and social rights and responsibilities.

The political organization of groups on the Northwest Coast most closely resembles that of chiefdoms. It does not fit the category neatly, however, and many suggest that its political structure—based on a village of independent houses, each with its own chief—is unique.

The diversity of groups in California is reflected in multiple kinds of political systems that were to be found there. Some groups are best classified as bands, others as tribes, and still others as chiefdoms.

The political structure of groups in the Southwest is another that is difficult to categorize. The settled farmers were most like chiefdoms, while the non-pueblo people who had less dependence on horticulture were most like tribes.

The Northeast exhibited a variety of political systems. The foragers from the north-east part of the area were organized as bands, while the horticultural groups exhibited characteristics of tribes and chiefdoms. Many of the groups were organized into confederacies, which were governing councils of various groups. The best known confederacy was the League of Iroquois.

In the Southeast, groups were organized as chiefdoms. There were many chiefdoms, each with at least one major town, claiming and using large amounts of land, and having populations in the thousands.

IDEOLOGY

Ideology includes people's belief systems, manifested in many ways such as in mythology and ritual. It typically shows strong correlations with other aspects of culture such as subsistence, art, and social and political systems. Among the Indigenous peoples of North America, for example, **culture heroes** are prominent in **myths**, and are often associated with introducing key subsistence resources to the group; while mythological figures often validate the kinds of social and political systems in place. Common features of North American Indigenous ideology are summarized in Table 5.5.

All ethnographically documented cultures had myths. The anthropological perspective on myths suggests that they have three main functions. One function is explanatory, insofar as myths explain both the natural and cultural worlds, such as features of the physical landscape and how and why cultural patterns originated. Another function is educational, such as in the retellings that are used to teach about culture history, customs, and values. The third function is entertainment, insofar as the myths often provide the basis of performance. The myths of the Indigenous peoples of North America, for example, were often played out in costume and involved considerable dance, song, and humor.

TABLE 5.5

Features of the Ideology of the Indigenous Peoples of North America

COMMON BELIEFS

Afterlife
The deceased passed to another world. Some believed in reincarnation.

Animism
Plants, animals, and other inanimate phenomena had spirits.

Ghosts
The spirit of a dead person remained nearby for some time.

Guardian Spirits
Guardian spirits that bestowed power to individuals were usually obtained during a vision quest.

Shamanism
Some individuals had a special relationship with the spirit world, which they would use for the benefit of individuals and the larger community.

Sweat lodges
Sweatbaths produced a spiritual cleansing.

COMMON FEATURES AND CHARACTERS OF MYTHS

Cannibals
The myths of many Indigenous groups featured cannibals.

Culture heroes
Many myths featured beings responsible for creating important aspects of the natural and cultural worlds, such as harnessing the sun and discovering how to grow crops.

Floods
Myths of many different groups involved floods.

Transformers
Beings that changed the animate and inanimate world are very common. One of the most common transformers is "Old Man," who is often credited with making changes to the world so that it could be occupied by humans.

Tricksters
Tricksters are usually culture heroes and transformers as well. They usually provide a positive benefit, but it is unintended. The most well-known trickster is Coyote.

WELL-KNOWN, BUT AREA-SPECIFIC FEATURES OF IDEOLOGY

Kachina
Kachinas are spirits of the dead, represented by masks and dolls among some Southwest groups.

Kiva
Sacred ceremonial structures often built partly underground, symbolizing the womb of Mother Earth. Common in the Southwest.

Kokopelli
Kokopelli meant different things to different people, but was often considered sacred to Indigenous peoples, especially those of the Southwest. He was often depicted in art with a hunchback and playing a flute. For some he represented a deity, a fertility symbol, or a shaman. Some believed him to be a trickster.

Raven
Raven was a prominent trickster of the Northwest Coast and adjoining culture areas.

Sedna
An important character in the Arctic, Sedna was recognized as being primarily responsible for providing food and clothing to the Inuit.

Sun Dance
Most groups had sacred ceremonies. Perhaps the best known was the sun dance, common to groups of the Plains.

Windigo
Groups in the Northeast had stories about Windigo, giant cannibals roaming the forests.

Every group has an origin myth. Origin myths routinely involve a time before the existence of humans in their present form, sometimes known as mythic time. Often there were creatures that were human-like but not quite human, and these are sometimes referred to as pre-humans or animal-people in the retelling of these stories. Time sequences are generally vague or non-existent in origin myths, although some have specific sequences. Hopi origin myths, for example, describe three previous worlds before the present one; and Navajo myths describe four.

There were two broad kinds of origin myths. One type usually involved a pre-human world in which human-like creatures must make their way through various levels of an underworld, or are trapped in some other way, with a culture hero often clearing the final hurdle. Such is the case in Haida mythology, for example, where the first people were locked in a giant clamshell until it was opened by **Raven** (depicted in Figure 3.1).

The other broad theme of origin myths involves the original people floating in waters that covered the earth. A culture hero successfully dives beneath the water and brings back mud to form an island that eventually grows in size and can support plants and animals. One version, common among groups of the Northeast, involves the placement of mud on the back of a turtle that eventually grows into what is now recognized as North America (and thus the term "Turtle Island"—often used by Indigenous peoples in place of North America).

Many myths involved **transformers**; origin myths typically describe beings that prepare the earth for humans. Bastian and Mitchell (2004, 208) describe them as follows:

> Many of the transformers in Native American mythology were individuals who were active in changing or reforming the earth and getting it ready for the coming of animals and humans. Often the transformer changed the shape of the land, set the mountains and lakes in their places, and taught humans and animals how they should live.

It is common for various myths of a single group to include many different transformers. While one transformer, for example, may prepare the earth in general for humans, specific features of the landscape—such as specific mountaintops or rock outcroppings—are often attributed to other transformers who came along after the original transformer, creating the features from other inanimate or animate things, including people. It is not unusual, for example, for attributes of the landscape to be explained as a human being turned into a stone outcrop, a mountaintop, or some other prominent physical feature. Some transformers have the ability to transform themselves into whatever they desire, animate or inanimate, and then back again at will. Transformers are usually culture heroes. They are also often, but not always, **tricksters**.

Trickster is a common character in the mythology of the Indigenous peoples of North America, and has been the subject of considerable anthropological study. One of the seminal works was by anthropologist Paul Radin ([1956] 1969) who described Trickster among North American groups as follows:

> Trickster is at one and the same time creator and destroyer, giver and negator, he who dupes others and who is always duped himself. He wills nothing consciously. At all times he is constrained to behave as he does from impulses over which he has no control. He knows neither good or evil yet is responsible for both. He possesses no values, moral or social, is at the mercy of his passions and appetites, yet through his actions all values come into being.

Indigenous myths typically include at least a few different tricksters, and their exploits are often humorous. Some are more predominant than others. Well-known tricksters include Manabozho (or Nanabush or Winabojo) in the Northeast; Rabbit (or Hare) in the Southeast; Spider on the Plains; and Raven on the Northwest Coast. Kokopelli is a well-known character in the myths of peoples of the Southwest; he is often described as a trickster, but not by all. While many tricksters are specific to one or two culture areas, others are more broadly featured in the myths of peoples across the continent. The most well-known trickster among North American Indigenous groups is **Coyote**. Bastian and Mitchell (2004, 76–77) describe Coyote as follows:

> Coyote is a complex, contradictory, and colourful figure that exists in virtually all of Native American cultural traditions.... The prototypical trickster, he is at times deceitful, dishonest, cunning, shrewd, irreverent,

curious, lazy, unpredictable, gluttonous, cruel, erotic, lecherous, clownish, or stupid. He frequently suffers from the consequences of his own mischief. Coyote is sometimes an animal, sometimes a man who can be either old and ugly or young and handsome. Magically powerful, he is able to create and transform, and often proves indestructible.

A belief in spirits was likely shared among all groups. In addition to recognizing a human spirit, it was common for Indigenous peoples to believe that many or all plants and animals also had spirits, a concept known as **animism**. Many groups extended this to include beliefs that inanimate things—such as lakes, mountains, rivers, and sometimes other natural phenomena such as unmodified rocks or manufactured artifacts—had spirits. This belief system was reflected in many ways, such as foragers ritually thanking their prey for giving themselves up.

Many groups also believed in the existence of guardian spirits, which helped individuals throughout their lives, often bestowing power on them. Members of some groups looked for spiritual guidance through a ritual widely known as a **vision quest**. Vision quests were typically carried out in solitude and after puberty, mostly by males, but also among females in some groups. The guardian spirit would manifest itself to the individual during the quest. Vision quests typically involved the individual putting themselves into an altered state of consciousness to obtain the vision and receive its power. In addition to isolation, this usually involved fasting, sleeplessness, and physical exertion. Some individuals had to make multiple vision quests before obtaining their guardian spirit. In some Indigenous societies, details of the visions were suppressed by the individuals receiving them. Through the subsequent actions of the individual, it would become apparent to others which guardian spirit had manifested itself to the individual and conferred its power on him or her. In other groups, however, the identity of the guardian spirit was made explicit through imagery, song, and dance.

Guardian spirits and vision quests were an effective way of linking the pre-mythic times with the present; they incorporated entities of ancient times with the present in the form of guardian spirits. Guardian spirits were often characters told in myths. According to Elmendorf (1977), when describing the vision quest as a ritual,

> … power was obtained from extra-human sources, conceptually connected with a prehuman mythic world, maintained and controlled through ritual practices and used to serve human ends. Aboriginally, the principal source of power was a class of animistic entities, the guardian spirits.

All groups had religious specialists, commonly known as shamans. In historic times, they had also been known as medicine men. Shamans were usually male, although female shamans existed as well. They had a special ability to deal with the mythical and spirit worlds. They could obtain this ability through training, a special encounter (such as during a vision quest), or both. Shamans acted as intermediaries between humans and supernatural beings. Their responsibilities included interpreting events and leading or performing religious rituals for the community, such as rituals ensuring successful hunting expeditions, warring expeditions, or harvests. They also diagnosed and treated illnesses related to spiritualism, such as soul loss. A shaman almost always acted on behalf of the community or its individuals. In the case of soul loss, for example, a shaman might have visited the spirit world to retrieve the soul.

Many groups incorporated sweat lodges into their belief systems. These were typically small, domed structures that could accommodate up to a dozen individuals and were constructed of poles covered with vegetation, mats, or animal skins. Rocks heated in a fire outside the structure would be brought in and water would be poured over them, creating steam. Sweatbaths were commonly considered to provide spiritual cleansing for individuals and they were also used in rituals for larger group activities, such as foraging.

Interacting with the spiritual world often involved entering an altered state of consciousness. Shamans were often specialists in this, but most others could do it as well, such as when they went on vision quests. Fasting, sleeplessness, exertion, drums, flutes, and chanting would all help to achieve an altered state of consciousness. Some groups also used hallucinogenic drugs. Where available, for example, some were able to use **peyote**, which comes from a cactus. Tobacco was used in ceremonies and religious rituals by some groups, particularly those from the Plains and eastern regions.

THE ARTS

Arts, both visual and performing, were pervasive among Indigenous groups. However, art was not considered as a separate component of culture like it is in many contemporary societies. It is likely that the Indigenous peoples would have appreciated the aesthetics of fine art, but that was likely not its primary function for them.

Anthropologists recognize several kinds of visual arts among Indigenous peoples, including two-dimensional artistic depictions such as paintings on wood, pottery, stone, animal hides, or other materials. Three-dimensional sculptures were created in any of several different materials such as stone, clay, bone, and wood. Woven designs on textiles and baskets are now also considered to be art.

Although arts were common in all Indigenous groups, the quantity and quality varied. Typically the generalized foragers, such as those existing in the Arctic, Subarctic, Great Basin, and Plains areas, had less art than other groups. Art may have been the most pervasive among Northwest Coast groups, wherein almost every kind of material culture they had—including houses, clothing, and everyday artifacts—were frequently painted or carved, often symbolizing their descent groups. As well, totem poles and other forms of wood sculpture were abundant in many of the Northwest Coast villages.

Performing arts were characteristic among all groups. They all had music and dancing, and drums, rattles, and flutes were common. Singing was a part of many people's daily lives, as well. Large gatherings of these groups usually featured many performances.

In most cases, both the visual and performing arts were strongly correlated with ideology and social organization. Supernatural beings and myths were often depicted in performances at public events. Similarly, much visual art depicted symbols of lineages and clans, and the rights to specific dances and songs were often tied to specific kinship and descent groups.

Visual arts were often created to show identity, both personal and within a group. For example, individuals in some groups would often paint their faces or have tattoos to express their personal identity. Some individuals decorated their personal belongings with images of their guardian spirit. In culture areas where lineages and clans were important, art often identified an individual's or group's descent group. This included designs on clothing, housing, and other material culture.

HEALTH AND HEALING

The Indigenous peoples of North America at about AD 1500 were likely fairly healthy. This would probably be attributable to their generally nutritious diet, hygienic lifestyle, and knowledge of natural medicines.

More than 2,500 plant species were used by the Indigenous peoples of North America as medicines (see Box 5.1). Many plants were used for multiple ailments. Moerman (2009) points out that only 55 plants were used for cancer treatment, likely due to the rarity of the disease at AD 1500. There are more 523 kinds of eye medicine, on the other hand, which is probably due to the problems caused by many groups having open fires inside their houses.

Indigenous peoples generally recognized differences between physical and spiritual illnesses. Physical illnesses could be treated by any knowledgeable member of the group. Besides knowledge of medicinal plants, peoples were generally skilled at fixing or resetting broken or dislocated limbs, and at treating infected gum and teeth through cauterization.

Spiritual illnesses were usually treated by a shaman, and often involved sweatbathing as a form of spiritual cleansing. Sometimes the shaman would enter the spirit world on behalf of the individual in an attempt to diagnose and cure the illness.

TECHNOLOGY AND MATERIAL CULTURE

The Indigenous peoples of North America had highly sophisticated technology and material culture. Subsistence technology included highly developed and complex techniques for hunting large animals on land and in the sea, both cooperatively and individually. Large land animals were hunted with bows and arrows, hand-thrown spears, and **atlatls**. For sea mammals, harpoons were often used. Some birds, small animals, and fish were sometimes captured in nets. Fish were taken with spears, hook-and-line methods, traps, nets, and weirs. Indigenous groups often modified the landscape through deliberate burning to create a suitable environment for their preferred plant and animal food sources. Some groups even modified intertidal zones to enhance shellfish populations. Groups knew the basic principles of horticulture, such as which plants grow best together (e.g., corn, beans, and squash).

The construction of stone tools was highly developed, as were weaving textiles made from both plant and animal (e.g., goat and sheep) fibers. Basket-making techniques were also highly sophisticated, whether they were made from bark or woven materials. Woven baskets were often made with such a tight weave that they could hold liquids. Wood technology among some groups was likely among the most developed in the world. It was common among Northwest Coast groups, for example, to have the four sides of a wooden box created by a single piece (i.e., bending cedar at 90-degree angles to form the four sides). Pottery technology was highly developed and widespread among sedentary groups; it didn't make much sense to have pottery if you were mobile.

Indigenous groups had multiple methods of cooking and preservation. Common cooking techniques included roasting over a fire, boiling, steaming, and using earth ovens. Some groups that did not use pottery were able to add hot rocks to water in baskets, which would allow them to boil food without exposing the baskets to direct fire. Preservation was commonly accomplished by drying or smoking.

Watercrafts were widespread among these groups. Both small and larger ocean-going canoes were widely used on the west coast; kayaks and larger boats were common in the Arctic; and smaller watercrafts were typical in many other places. In areas without large trees, boats made of bark or animal skins were common.

Clothing depended on what was suitable in regards to climate, as well as on what was available. Those in cold environments usually made their clothes from the skins and fur of large mammals. Those with considerable vegetation often wove their clothing from plants. Many used animal skins.

Jewelry was common, and was often made of exotic materials that came from some vast distances away, such as shells and rare stones. Some of these items would have traveled thousands of miles.

TRADITIONAL LIFEWAYS IN A GLOBAL PERSPECTIVE

Some of the characteristics of the traditional lifeways of the Indigenous peoples of North America are shared with other Indigenous peoples, and some others are distinctive.

The general kinds of settlement patterns associated with foragers and horticulturalists, for example, were and continue to be shared among foragers and horticulturalists around the world. Although the specific features of habitation structures may differ, it is the norm that foragers build temporary shelters while horticulturalists build more permanent structures.

None of the subsistence strategies exhibited by North American groups before the arrival of Europeans were unique. Generalized foraging, specialized foraging, and horticulture had all occurred elsewhere. Other forms of subsistence, such as **pastoralism** and **agriculture**, had occurred elsewhere but not yet in North America.

Most of the social and political systems exhibited by the Indigenous peoples of North America have also been common elsewhere. However, the recognition of the "house" as the primary social and economic unit among Northwest Coast groups, and the political confederacies of groups from the Northeast, may be unique.

The general ideology of North American Indigenous groups was shared with many other Indigenous groups around the world. Animism, for example, is a very common belief among Indigenous peoples. Many groups outside of North America also have beliefs in transformers, tricksters, and guardian spirits. The details in beliefs, myths, and culture heroes, however, are usually substantially different. Likewise, shamans are common outside of North America.

The existence of visual and performing arts among Indigenous peoples is common among peoples everywhere. The details, however, remain distinct. Some of the art forms of North American Indigenous groups, especially those of the Northwest Coast, are often considered to be among the most sophisticated in the world. Similarly, the arts of many other groups are highly valued, as are traditional weaving, pottery, and basket making.

SUGGESTED READINGS

A good place to begin further reading on traditional lifeways is with the Smithsonian Institution's *Handbook of North American Indians*. Summaries of multiple groups, often written in the ethnographic present, are included in the volumes for each culture area.

Primary data on the traditional lifeways of the Indigenous peoples of North America exist in the hundreds of ethnographies widely available in book form from libraries. Summaries of some lifeways can be found in the Human Relations Area files (HRAF), which large or academic libraries often subscribe to.

More focused books include the edited volume *A Companion to the Anthropology of American Indians* (Biolsi 2008), which includes chapters on demography, religion, music, and art. For ethnobotany, two books by Daniel Moerman are recommended: *Native American Food Plants* (2010) and *Native American Medicinal Plants* (2009). For an overview of mythology, see the *Handbook of Native American Mythology* (Bastian and Mitchell 2004); and for an overview of art, see *Native North American Art* (Berlo and Phillips 1998).

SIX

UNDERSTANDING THE COLONIAL EXPERIENCE

INTRODUCTION

It would be hard to overestimate the impact of European peoples and policy on the Indigenous peoples and cultures of North America. This chapter considers the nature of these changes, their impacts, and the reactions to them. It does this with a clearly anthropological perspective, focused on culture change. To provide context, the chapter first includes a brief overview of the history of Europeans in North America. This is followed with overviews of the agents of colonialism-induced change to Indigenous populations and cultures; the processes of change; the nature of the changes to Indigenous peoples and cultures; and the reactions to these changes. The chapter covers the period from approximately AD 1500–2000. The twenty-first century is covered in Chapter 7.

CONTINENTAL DIPLOMACY IN NORTH AMERICA

The purpose of this section is to provide a framework for understanding the historical context in which Indigenous populations and cultures have changed since the time of Christopher Columbus.

"Continental diplomacy" is a polite way of describing the struggles for control of the lands, resources, and Indigenous peoples of North America, first by European countries and more recently by the governments of the United States and Canada. Diplomacy often invokes thoughts of peaceful negotiation to settle disputes, and while this did occur on occasion, it was often the case that violent conflict was involved on many levels—including battles between colonial nations; battles between colonial nations and Indigenous populations; and battles between European colonists and their

TABLE 6.1
Timeline of Continental Diplomacy in North America

Date	Event
AD 1000	The first European (Norse/Viking) settlements in North America.
Late 1400s	Christopher Columbus makes his first of multiple voyages to the Caribbean, setting the foundation for Spanish colonialism. Columbus never sets foot on mainland North America. Giovanni Caboto (John Cabot) reaches the Northeast, setting the foundation for British Colonialism.
1500s–1700s	European nations compete with each other for control of North American lands, resources, and Indigenous peoples. Following the American Revolution, continental diplomacy continues, with the British and French maintaining control throughout much of what are now the United States and Canada. There is limited recognition of Indigenous rights. European influence is mostly restricted to the east and southern parts of the continent. Much of the west and north is considered "Indian Territory."
1800s	Continental diplomacy continues, with Americans and Europeans continuing expansion into "Indian Territory." Following 1867, when Canada becomes a country, Canada and the United States become the major political forces, enacting many strategies including violence, negotiation, relocation, and assimilation acts, policies, and practices to expand their domination over the lands, resources, and Indigenous peoples. These actions are often rationalized by ideology (e.g., manifest destiny). Relatively little attention is given to Indigenous rights.
1900s	American and Canadian dominance continues through early parts of the century, with relatively little value placed on Indigenous rights. In the latter half of the century American and Canadian governments increasingly recognize Indigenous rights.

home countries (e.g., the American Revolution). A brief summary of continental diplomacy is presented in Table 6.1.

The history of Europeans in North America can be accurately said to have begun about 1,000 years ago with the Norse (Viking) settlements in Greenland and eastern Canada (Newfoundland). While the impact on Indigenous populations in those areas was likely severe, those incursions are widely considered to have had relatively little impact on the Indigenous peoples elsewhere, and are thus not usually considered significant when discussing the impacts of Europeans on the Indigenous peoples of the continent in its entirety.

The late 1400s set the stage for significant European-induced change on the peoples and cultures of Indigenous North America. The European discovery of the Americas is usually associated with the AD 1492 landing of Christopher Columbus in what is now recognized as the Caribbean. Sailing on behalf of Spain, Columbus made multiple voyages to the Caribbean but never actually set foot on the lands now recognized as Mexico, the United States, and Canada. Ultimately, however, the Spanish conquest of the Caribbean, beginning with Columbus, spread to Mesoamerica and South America, and then into the southern portions of North America in the sixteenth century—especially the Southeast, Southwest, and California.

While Columbus's incursions into the Caribbean set the stage for Spanish **colonialism**, it wasn't long after that claims were made by others. In 1497, Giovanni Caboto (John Cabot) arrived in the Northeast, setting the stage for British colonialism; and a short time later, in the early 1500s, the French started to make their claims in what is now recognized as the St. Lawrence River system.

Over the next few hundred years the British, French, and Spanish struggled for control of the lands, resources, and Indigenous peoples of the continent. Other countries attempted colonialization as well. Denmark successfully colonized Greenland; Sweden and the Netherlands established colonies in the Northeast; and Russia controlled much of Alaska. On a continent-wide basis, however, the story of continental diplomacy primarily revolves around Britain, France, Spain, and the Indigenous nations.

There is no one model to characterize the approaches and strategies that the Europeans and their descendants used to fulfill their goals of colonialization. Colonialism is often used to describe the process of a people from a European nation, with the support of that nation, going to a land occupied by Indigenous peoples and subjugating and dominating them. It usually involves a claim by the European nation, extending authority over the lands, resources, and people. Two major kinds of colonialism are commonly recognized: **exploitation colonialism** and **settler colonialism**. Both kinds occurred in North America.

Exploitation colonialism typically has the primary goal of extracting resources with relatively few colonists; in other words, the notion of taking what resources are already there with the least amount of effort. Settler colonialism, on the other hand, typically involves a larger number of colonists who are intent on creating new settlements and using their knowledge to produce new resources, such as with farming.

The activities of the Spanish, British, and French each exhibited aspects of both exploitation and settler colonialism, although there were substantial differences in the focus of each. Early Spanish incursions were primarily examples of exploitation colonialism, and they were often violent. In addition to taking riches, they also frequently made slaves of the Indigenous peoples. Both the French and British were involved in exploitation colonialization, focusing on the fur trade. The French and British were also involved in settler colonialization, however, with initial colonies in what are now Canada and the United States.

Throughout the sixteenth, seventeenth, and eighteenth centuries, there was considerable competition among the British, Spanish, and French for the resources of North America. While the Spanish continued to dominate the south, the British maintained dominance in much of what are now parts of eastern Canada and the north-east United States. The French maintained dominance in parts of what is now eastern Canada, as well as in the St. Lawrence River system and much of the central part of the continent down to what is now Louisiana.

Eventually the influence of the Spanish waned, leaving the British and French colonists (and the administrators of the colonies on behalf of the European homelands) to battle for control. This conflict was focused in the eastern part of the continent. Here, the Europeans were battling both with the Indigenous populations and with each other.

When the United States was created in the late 1700s, and when Canada was created almost a century later, those countries replaced the European governments in diplomatic relations with the Indigenous groups.

PRINCIPAL POLICIES, PRACTICES, AND AGENTS OF CHANGE
There were many causes of change to the Indigenous peoples and cultures of North America that began in the late 1400s. The principal agents of these changes are listed in Table 6.2.

The early French and British explorers of the sixteenth century tended to have little impact on the Indigenous peoples. The Spanish, on the other hand, had devastating impacts. Following and coinciding with their conquering and pillaging of South America and Mesoamerica, the Spanish sought riches from the Indigenous peoples of North America, hoping to find caches of gold and other treasures similar to what they had recovered further south. Upon finding far less riches in North America, the Spanish resorted to massacres and the taking of slaves. This was primarily restricted to areas of the Southeast and Southwest.

The fur traders, who were mostly British and French, generally brought no ill-will towards the Indigenous peoples. Although conflict did occur on occasion, their relationship could generally be characterized as relatively peaceful. For the fur traders, contact with the Indigenous peoples was a business, and they had no explicit desires to alter the Indigenous cultures beyond trade; however, this still happened on occasion. In some cases, fur traders may have inadvertently introduced fatal diseases to Indigenous populations, for example. The fur trade also led to changes in subsistence and settlement patterns as many groups began to focus more on hunting

TABLE 6.2
Major Agents of Change to Indigenous Peoples and Cultures since
AD 1500

- The Early Explorers (Spanish, British, and French)
- Disease (introduced by Europeans)
- The Fur Traders (mostly British and French)
- Colonial Governments (mostly Spanish, British, and French)
- Settlers (mostly British and French)
- Missionaries (Spanish, British, and French)
- Boarding Schools (run by religious orders, supported by the government)
- Governments of the United States and Canada
- Indigenous Peoples

and trapping animals for their fur, which they could trade with the Europeans. Some groups moved their villages closer to the fur trade posts, and some groups were able to reposition themselves as intermediaries between more remote Indigenous groups and the European fur traders. The trade items that Indigenous groups received in exchange, including metal tools, blankets, firearms, and alcohol, all led to changes in the economic and social spheres of their culture, as well.

Colonial administrators and more recent governments have had enormous impacts on Indigenous populations and cultures. Some of the most important proclamations, policies, practices, and acts are listed in Table 6.3.

The Royal Proclamation of 1763 was issued by the British monarch King George III (see Appendix 4) and was integral to the formation of Aboriginal policy in subsequent American and Canadian governments. The proclamation was issued to provide a sense of order between British subjects and Indigenous peoples in North America. It recognized the rights and lands of Indigenous groups and established the system of surrendering those rights and lands by treaty. Indian policy of colonial and subsequent governments in the United States and Canada echoed the proclamation, but not without violations. The vagueness of parts of the proclamation, for example, led to different interpretations of rights and lands. In general, American Indian policy was more accepting of the rights of Indigenous peoples than the governments of what is now Canada.

The acts listed in Table 6.3 provide only a small sample of the government policies, practices, and acts affecting Indigenous peoples in the United States. In Canada, the Indian Act is the legislation of principal importance, along with some important court decisions and the Constitution, which affirms Aboriginal rights. There are many more important pieces of legislation in the United States. According to Brock (2008, 276),

TABLE 6.3
Important Acts of Governments Affecting the Indigenous Peoples of North America

Act	Description
BOTH THE UNITED STATES AND CANADA	
The Royal Proclamation of 1763	The proclamation established the framework that has governed relations in both the United States and Canada from the late 1700s to the present.
CANADA	
The Indian Act (1876)	The Indian Act is the key federal act that governs Indigenous peoples in Canada. It has been revised several times since 1876.
The Canadian Constitution (1982)	The Canadian Constitution recognizes and affirms the rights of the Indigenous peoples of Canada.
UNITED STATES	
Indian Removal Act (1830)	This act led to the forced removal of many Indigenous peoples from the east to reservations west of the Mississippi.
The Dawes Act (1887)	Also known as the General Allotment Act, this act caused the division of communal reservation lands into privately held parcels, effectively leading to the breakdown of traditional systems and reducing the amount of lands controlled by Indians.
Indian Citizenship Act (1924)	The granting of US citizenship was piecemeal before 1924. Under this act, Indians did not have to apply to become US citizens, nor did they have to give up their Indian status.
The Indian Reorganization Act (1934)	Also known as the Wheeler-Howard Act, this act renewed communal control of land and resources and provided for limited forms of sovereignty.

American legislation "comprises over 5,000 federal statutes, 2,000 federal court opinions, and nearly 400 ratified treaties and agreements."

The Indian Removal Act (1830) was designed to free up land desired by those of European descent in the eastern part of the continent. It was hoped that many Indigenous people would voluntarily move west, and some did. Many did not go voluntarily, however, which led to much devastation. The well-known Trail of Tears was one effect of the act. In the late 1800s, the US army forcibly marched approximately 15,000 Cherokee from their homelands more than 800 miles west to be resettled. Approximately 4,000 died along the way.

The Dawes Act was seen by many as a way to both encourage Indigenous peoples to become more like Europeans through private land ownership, and to break down the concept of communal tribal ownership. It also freed up Indian-controlled lands for purchase by those of European descent, resulting in a net loss of lands for use by Indigenous people.

The Indian Citizenship Act was also seen as a way of encouraging Indigenous peoples to become more European-like and to participate as full citizens of the United States. The Indian Reorganization Act sought to reverse or at least slow the loss of lands and to restore tribal control.

Governments also legitimized military action against the Indigenous peoples, which resulted in the loss of many thousands of Indigenous lives. Some refer to the military actions against Indigenous groups in the United States as the "Indian Wars." Some have also suggested that some military leaders deliberately passed blankets infected with smallpox to Indigenous peoples in an attempt at genocide. While historical records show the idea was considered, there is no evidence that the plan was acted upon.

Settlers were another agent of significant change. Often, colonial governments would enact legislation to benefit the settlers of European descent. This frequently resulted in Indigenous people being forbidden to maintain their traditional subsistence and settlement patterns. Settlers also often undertook their own massacres of Indigenous peoples; this was especially prevalent in California.

Christian missionaries generally had little impact until the devastation of Indigenous peoples and cultures was near. As populations dwindled and cultures continued to suffer from negative impacts, some Indigenous peoples eventually began to accept the teaching of the missionaries. An Indigenous perspective on the works of missionaries with peoples from the Northwest Coast is provided by Gloria Cranmer Webster (1992, 29):

> The introduction of Christianity must have been a confusing time for our people. At the same time missionaries like Hall were preaching "Thou shall not steal," settlers were helping themselves to large tracts of land.... While Hall was telling the people that "It is better to give than to receive," he was also telling them that lavish gift-giving at potlatches was sinful and heathenish. With all the mixed messages the missionaries were giving the local people, it is no wonder that there were few converts. People had difficulty making sense of it all.

Governments and Christian religious orders came together in the 1800s to establish schools for Indigenous children. The governments made it law that Indigenous children attend the schools, which were operated by the

FIGURE 6.1 US School for Indians. Located at Pine Ridge, South Dakota, with a tipi camp in the foreground, 1891. (Photo courtesy of the Library of Congress.)

religious orders. They were called boarding schools in the United States and residential schools in Canada. In both countries, children were forcibly removed from their parents and home communities to become indoctrinated in the ways of Non-Indigenous, Christian society. In practice, this meant that not only were the children removed from their families and communities, but they were taught that Indigenous cultures were bad; they were forbidden to speak their own Indigenous languages; they were given very little academic education; they were indoctrinated into Christianity; and they were often physically, emotionally, and sexually abused. Some religious orders have publicly apologized for the actions, and in 2008 the Canadian government apologized as well (see Appendix 5).

The Indigenous peoples themselves may also be viewed as agents of change. Those involved in the fur trade, for example, were willing participants and quick to adopt such things as metal tools; and many groups were quick to adopt the use of horses, first introduced to North America by the Spaniards in the 1500s, into their cultures.

TABLE 6.4
Anthropological Terminology and Concepts of Culture Change

Accommodation	The acceptance of the cultural traditions of subordinate groups by a dominant one.
Acculturation	A dominant culture forcing their culture on subordinate peoples.
Assimilation	A subordinate culture being absorbed into a dominant culture.
Culture loss	An aspect of culture that is lost.
Ethnocide	Deliberate destruction of a culture.
Genocide	Deliberate destruction of a population.
Revitalization	A deliberate attempt to bring back, or otherwise celebrate, traditional lifeways.
Syncretism	A mixing of cultural traditions to create a new form.

PROCESSES OF CHANGE

Anthropologists have several terms and concepts to describe and explain culture change. Some of these are listed in Table 6.4.

The term accommodation in some ways describes the current situation in relations between governments and Indigenous peoples. After various attempts at assimilation over recent centuries, governments in both the United States and Canada have now taken an approach of accommodation, supporting Indigenous groups' desires to maintain their own distinct cultures within the larger North American society.

Acculturation and **assimilation** are the dominant processes that governments and many other non-Indigenous peoples have supported, and many continue to support (though Indigenous peoples and anthropologists generally do not). **Eurocentrism** has long dominated the basic attitudes of Europeans and those of European descent, and many sincerely believe that indoctrinating the Indigenous peoples in the ways of Europeans and their descendants would be a good thing. Many of the laws and policies enacted by governments may be viewed as instruments of acculturation and assimilation.

The loss of some cultural traditions through legislation or other actions is viewed by some as attempts at ethnocide. Many aspects of traditional lifeways were outlawed in the past, such as the potlatch among Northwest Coast groups and the Sun Dance on the Plains.

Syncretism properly describes a mixing of traditions. This is clearly evident in the mixing of religious traditions among Indigenous groups. While many have adopted Christianity, for example, elements of traditional culture persist in their religious beliefs and ceremonies.

Revitalization describes many of the activities initiated by Indigenous peoples in North America over the last several decades. Beginning in the

1960s, revitalization of cultural traditions, especially in the forms of the arts and ideology, has become prominent.

The Indigenous Experience: Changes to Populations and Cultures

The impact of the European incursions into North America had severe repercussions on the continent's Indigenous peoples and cultures. Population loss was catastrophic for most groups; some culture areas lost more than 90 per cent of their Indigenous populations. About 200 Indigenous languages became extinct. Subsistence strategies, diets, settlement patterns, housing, social systems, political systems, ideology, art, technology, and material culture all changed substantially.

Anthropologists know that in most instances, a change in one aspect of culture inevitably has repercussions throughout the entire culture. With European colonization, however, there was a multi-pronged approach to culture change. Population loss was extreme, primarily due to disease and conflict. Changes in languages were partially a reflection of population loss but also of government policies and practices preventing the use of Indigenous languages. Traditional subsistence and settlement patterns were, in many cases, impossible to maintain in the context of conflicts, non-Indigenous expansionism, and government policies and practices. Non-indigenous governments disregarded traditional forms of social and political organization. And, finally, European missionaries approached culture change through ideology.

Population Loss

European incursions led to severe population loss among Indigenous populations. On a continent-wide basis, the primary agents of loss were European-introduced diseases to which the populations had little or no natural immunity, or access to preventative vaccinations. Diseases that caused significant mortality included smallpox, measles, influenza, diphtheria, typhus, cholera, malaria, yellow fever, and whooping cough. In many cases, due to Indigenous economic and social networks, infected populations unknowingly would have infected other groups that had not yet had direct contact with Europeans. Populations also suffered dramatic declines due to massacres and other conflicts.

Anthropologist Douglas Ubelaker (2006) calculated the total loss of population among Indigenous groups at about 78 per cent, although the differences in percentage and the dates at which the populations reached their lowest points differ significantly between culture areas. These differences are illustrated along with the averages for each area in Table 6.5. There

TABLE 6.5

Indigenous Population Loss Resulting from European Colonialization
of North America (based on Ubelaker 2006)

Culture Area	Approximate Date of Nadir (lowest population)	Per cent Loss
Arctic	1900	53
Subarctic	1900	30
Northwest Coast	1910	84
California	1940	96
Southwest	1900	72
Great Basin	1930	68
Plateau	1890	78
Plains	1900	69
Northeast	1900	77
Southeast	1800	90
TOTAL		78

would also have been significant differences within individual groups in regards to both the loss of population and the date at which the population reached its lowest number—these dates, according to Ubelaker, range from 1650 to 1985.

Change to Languages

It is widely accepted that about 200 Indigenous languages have become extinct over the past 500 years, representing about 50 per cent of the original number of languages spoken when European colonialization began. The severe population loss from disease and violence is partially to blame for this, but there are other factors as well. Governments, primarily through assimilation policies and in particular through the residential and boarding schools, deliberately tried to rid the Indigenous peoples of their languages. The breakdown of social systems that led to Indigenous peoples leaving their traditional territories, reservations, and reserves to find employment also led to the loss of language, as those joining the labor forces had fewer and sometime no speakers of the same language with which to communicate.

Change to Subsistence Strategies and Diet

For most Indigenous groups, change in subsistence strategies and diet was inevitable, but the degree of change varied substantially. Some change was voluntary, such as with some foragers who began to shift towards the

FIGURE 6.2 Plains Woman on Horse Pulling a Travois, 1908. (Photo by Edward S. Curtis. Courtesy of the Library of Congress.)

trapping of animals that could be traded with Europeans. Mostly, however, change in subsistence strategies and diet was dictated by population loss and changes in settlement, as well as by social and political patterns.

For all groups, population loss was severe, and it became impossible to maintain subsistence practices that required substantial numbers of people working cooperatively. This impacted almost every kind of subsistence activity, since most were communal. Changes in settlement patterns, dictated to large extent by European colonialization (e.g., warfare, treaties, reservations, forced relocation), prevented Indigenous peoples from fully using their traditional territories and inevitably resulted in changes in subsistence, since it was no longer feasible to maintain the traditional systems where the resources were different. In the social and political spheres, resistance to non-Indigenous peoples (and other Indigenous groups who at times were their allies) caused a reallocation of priorities, and it is likely that subsistence and diet changed because of this as well. Subsistence and diet were also impacted by increased competition for resources; when Europeans started coming in significant numbers, it created stress on the continent's resources.

FIGURE 6.3 Indigenous Gold Miners. An Indigenous group mining with sluice boxes and gold pans in the Plateau culture area, *c.* 1890. (Photo courtesy of Royal BC Museum, BC Archives. BCARS D-06815.)

In some cases, the focus on specific subsistence activities changed as a result of European-based technology. The introduction of firearms, for example, likely led many foraging groups to increase their focus on big-game hunting. This was perhaps most evident in the Plains region, where firearms and the introduction of horses likely led to an increased focus on buffalo hunting.

Environmental changes due to the activities of Non-Indigenous peoples also had an impact on subsistence and diet. Non-Indigenous farmers, ranchers, and miners altered the natural environment, depleting many of the resources upon which Indigenous peoples depended.

Generally, most Indigenous groups were able to maintain their traditional subsistence strategies and diet until either the resources had been depleted by European activities or until access to their traditional lands was impeded—by being displaced, for example. Government assimilation policies and practices often encouraged or demanded European-style farming. Ultimately, as Indigenous peoples became increasingly marginalized and restricted from their traditional lands, a more European kind of diet prevailed. For most groups there simply was no option.

As it became increasingly difficult for Indigenous peoples to maintain their traditional economies, many turned to work in the emerging industries such as mining, logging, fishing, ranching, and transportation. Some were able to create and develop their own enterprises, but there were many obstacles, such as being denied access to water and lands. The kinds of inducements for settlement and businesses that were granted to Europeans, such as the free use of land, were rarely available to the Indigenous peoples. Consequently, many Indigenous peoples had no option but to work for wages as laborers in businesses run by those of European descent.

While the changes brought by Europeans have made it impossible to maintain many of the traditional aspects of subsistence and diet among most groups, there are some who have maintained core elements of their traditional economies. Many Indigenous peoples of the Arctic, Subarctic, Plateau, and Northwest Coast, for example—particularly those in rural areas—still actively fish, hunt, and gather wild plants and animals. However, these groups now often incorporate contemporary technology, such as rifles, snowmobiles, and pick-up trucks, into their traditional practices.

Change to Settlement Patterns and Housing

Settlement patterns changed substantially in response to European incursions into the continent. For groups involved in economic trade with the Europeans, the change in settlement patterns was often initiated by the Indigenous groups themselves—for example, they might change their seasonal rounds to accumulate furs and other trade goods desirable to Europeans. In some cases, Indigenous groups moved their settlements closer to trading forts, and some groups were able to become more sedentary by manipulating their role as intermediaries between Europeans and other Indigenous groups. As colonialism continued, it became increasingly difficult for Indigenous peoples to maintain their traditional territories and seasonal rounds. This was due to a multitude of reasons, including severe population loss, conflict with non-Indigenous peoples, forced relocation, treaties, the creation of the reservation and reserve systems, and increased economic marginalization that led to many migrating to urban areas for employment.

In pre-European times, most Indigenous groups had multiple sites that they would spend time at during the year. Colonialism resulted in significant loss of mobility, and thus a reduction in the number of settlement sites, for most groups.

Changes to settlement patterns often led to changes in housing. Many of the traditional forms of housing were appropriate for nomadic or semi-sedentary ways of life. Once Indigenous peoples became more sedentary, the temporary structures characteristic of their traditional lifeways no longer made much sense and were often given up. Those with more permanent kinds of structures were often keen to incorporate European materials into their housing. It was not uncommon, for example, to see traditional kinds of Indigenous housing incorporating glass windows and European-style doors.

Change to Social Systems

The significant loss of population led to severe impacts on the social systems of the Indigenous populations. As outlined in the previous chapter, kinship was a key component of many Indigenous populations, dictating rights, responsibilities, status, and leadership. In many contexts, it could be argued that kinship was what established the rules for societies and held them together. Kinship relations governed individual and group behavior and were manifested in economic, social, and political activities, as well as in material culture and ideology. Thus, significant population loss often led to the breakdown of social systems. Since Indigenous peoples did not have written languages, considerable knowledge about relations, rights, responsibilities, and more was lost as the carriers of those traditions died. For societies with hereditary leadership, for example, it was not always clear who should be the new leader following population loss. As people dispersed from traditional homelands, villages, and territories for myriad reasons relating to colonialism, the structures and relevance of nuclear families, extended families, lineages, and clans became less important.

Change to Political Systems

The political systems of Indigenous peoples changed in multiple ways. In some instances, alliances were formed between Indigenous groups in order to resist the European incursions. On the other hand, however, Indigenous groups were often sought as allies by the non-Indigenous groups; this consequently saw some groups becoming allies with the French and others becoming allies with the British. Some Indigenous groups fought on the side of the British while others fought alongside the colonists in the American Revolution. During the American civil war, some groups fought with the North and others with the Confederacy.

Ultimately, as the influence of non-Indigenous governments and their agents increased, the traditional forms of political organization in many groups were lost. Governments often reorganized traditional bands, tribes, and chiefdoms for administrative purposes, and in many cases this was not an accurate reflection of these groups' original political organization.

Change to Ideology

Belief systems were among the slowest components of Indigenous cultures to change over the past 500 years. Christian missionaries had a presence in North America since the earliest periods of colonialization, but their impact on changing Indigenous belief systems was largely slow and rarely complete. Many Indigenous peoples ultimately did become Christians, at least in name, but this often occurred only after significant population loss and changes to other components of culture. This was perhaps due to the loss of religious specialists in Indigenous societies, the failure of Indigenous peoples' own ideology to satisfactorily explain the devastation that was going on around them, and the coercive power, policies, and practices of the non-Indigenous governments.

Change to the Arts

Colonialization had multiple effects on the visual and performing arts. In some cultural areas the visual arts probably reached their peak after initial contact with the Europeans. Although not the primary focus of trade, the visual arts did become useful for producing trade items and some Indigenous peoples began to produce art strictly for trade. This was clearly the case in the Northwest Coast, for example; and their already sophisticated three-dimensional art carved from wood was produced more easily and quickly with the introduction of metal carving tools.

Performing arts, such as dancing and singing, often went underground. The reason for this was that non-Indigenous governments often banned ceremonies and rituals that they did not understand.

Because visual art produces a material record, anthropologists have a better idea of the changes that have occurred in that realm than they do of what occurred in the performing arts. Overall, the changes in visual arts do not appear significant. Changes in performing arts, however, remain much more speculative. It is likely that some stories, dances, songs, and more may have been lost forever due to the severe loss of population, regulations against such activities, and further breakdown in Indigenous communities caused by non-Indigenous governments and their agents.

Change to Technology and Material Culture

Indigenous peoples were often quick to adopt European technology and material culture. During the initial periods of colonialization, firearms, metal tools, and blankets in particular were adopted relatively quickly. In the Plains, once the horse was introduced, its use was quickly adopted by Indigenous peoples.

In some cases the changes in material culture may have occurred because they made sense from the perspective of Indigenous groups. Many could see, for example, the advantages of using metal pots as opposed to clay pots or baskets for cooking; using metal tools instead of tools manufactured from stone; and using horses. It should also be appreciated, however, that as Indigenous peoples lost their access to their traditional lands and resources, it became difficult to find the resources that were integral to the material culture. It should further be appreciated that since material culture was strongly correlated with settlement, housing, diet, social and political systems, and ideology, changes in those parts of culture were inevitably reflected in material culture. It did not make sense, for example, to maintain housing that was useful for particular seasonal activities when those activities were no longer taking place.

INDIGENOUS REACTIONS TO CHANGE

There have been several reactions to the change to Indigenous populations and cultures instigated by Europeans and their descendants (see Table 6.6).

Assaults on Indigenous cultures by those of European descent were by no means universally successful. Certainly some Indigenous peoples were willing partners in trade, for example, but the large-scale changes induced by non-Indigenous governments and people have largely been resisted by Indigenous peoples.

There are many historic records, for example, of Indigenous groups in various jurisdictions protesting to government officials in person. Some groups even ventured to Great Britain to protest to the British government. In some cases the protests were formalized, with official petitions being presented to the governments. The typical reaction to these protests and petitions has been one of inaction on the parts of governments.

Conflict and confrontations between Indigenous and non-Indigenous people have a long history. Mostly, Indigenous peoples have been defensive, arguing and supporting what they view as legal protection from incursions on their lands, resources, and rights (such as by the Royal proclamation treaties, and other agreements.) In the past, official "Indian Wars" between the US military and Indigenous groups, as well as smaller battles and massacres by the military, settlers, and others, led to tens of thousands of deaths from violent confrontations. Today, although not as frequent as they once were, violent confrontations still occur. One of the largest events of armed resistance in recent times occurred in 1990 in the community of Oka in the province of Quebec.

Often referred to as the Oka Crisis or the Standoff at Kanesatake, the

TABLE 6.6
Indigenous Reactions to Change

- Protests and Petitions
- Conflict and Confrontations
- Revitalization
- Negotiation
- Litigation
- Activism
- Advocacy
- Acceptance

standoff began when the town of Oka decided to expand a golf course into territory claimed by an Indigenous group. The result was a 78-day standoff between the Indigenous supporters and the Canadian military. According to Simpson (2011, 213), the standoff "saw the largest military deployment of force by a settler state since the 'Indian Wars' in what is now the United States, which are largely thought to have ended more than a century ago."

Negotiation has a long history in North America, including in the creation of treaties and other agreements. These agreements are an ongoing process. Since the 1990s in western Canada, for example, dozens of Indigenous groups have been negotiating modern-day treaties with governments.

Litigation has been a popular form of resistance for groups both in Canada and the United States. It extends back into the 1800s and continues today. Taking claims of Indigenous rights to court is commonplace in both countries.

Revitalization and activism both began in a significant way in the late 1960s. Many Indigenous peoples began to rediscover and celebrate their culture around that time, and this has continued to the present. Activism also became significant at this time, particularly the formation of the American Indian Movement, often abbreviated as AIM. The American Indian Movement was behind such well-known events in the 1970s as the occupation of Alcatraz, the occupation of the Bureau of Indian Affairs in Washington, DC, and the standoff at Wounded Knee.

Political advocacy is a relatively new force in the Indigenous political sphere. Groups such as the National Congress of the American Indian in the United States and the Assembly of First Nations in Canada have taken on the role of becoming advocates of a plethora of Indigenous issues on national scales, including those related to rights, identity, health, and education.

One reaction that is often not discussed is the acceptance of assimilation. Many Indigenous peoples have welcomed assimilation into non-

FIGURE 6.4 Standoff at Oka. Canadian soldier and Indigenous person come to face to face during Oka Crisis, 1990. (Photo © The Canadian Press / Shaney Komulainen. Reprinted by permission.)

Indigenous society. Robert B. Porter (2005), for example, suggests that for many generations there has been a gap between those Indigenous people who want to preserve their distinct existence and right of self-determination and those Indigenous peoples who want to assimilate into American society—and the gap is widening.

UNDERSTANDING THE COLONIAL EXPERIENCE IN A GLOBAL PERSPECTIVE

The processes and impacts of the colonial experience in North America are shared among many Indigenous groups around the world. North American groups share the most similarity with the groups that have also been subject to the colonial practices of the Spanish, British, and French. Many Indigenous groups in Mesoamerica and South America, for example, suffered similar brutality and massacres at the hands of the Spanish as did the Indigenous peoples of North America.

The Indigenous experience in Australia and New Zealand is probably the closest to that of the Indigenous peoples in North America; the policies, practices, and processes of the colonial governments were similar in these places. The reactions by the groups in question have also been similar.

SUGGESTED READINGS

There are many excellent sources on the Indigenous Peoples of North America during historic times. The *Handbook of North American Indians, Volume 4: Indian–White Relations,* edited by Wilcomb E. Washburn, provides dozens of good chapters written by scholars in the field.

Those interested in the forced assimilation of Indigenous peoples through schooling are directed to Adams (1995) regarding the experience in the United States; Miller (1996) regarding the experience in Canada; and A. Smith (2009) for a global perspective.

Other good sources for the colonial period include those by Scheiber and Mitchell (2010); Nabokov (1999); Porter (2005); Nichols (1998); Trigger and Washburn (1996); McNickle (1973); and Hill (2009).

SEVEN

CONTEMPORARY CONDITIONS, NATION-BUILDING, AND ANTHROPOLOGY

INTRODUCTION

The chapter begins with an overview of reports and studies relating to the contemporary state of Indigenous economies, health, social conditions, and education. This is followed by a section on nation-building and an overview of the nature of contemporary anthropology when it is done in association with the Indigenous peoples of North America.

OVERVIEW OF THE ECONOMIC AND SOCIAL CONDITIONS OF THE INDIGENOUS PEOPLES OF NORTH AMERICA

Many anthropologists and other social scientists have studied the economic and social conditions of the Indigenous peoples of North America in both historic and contemporary times. One of the most comprehensive projects on this topic in recent years has been the Harvard Project on American Indian Economic Development, begun in 1987. Based on hundreds of studies done over two decades in consultation with Indigenous groups of the United States, the Harvard Project published a survey of their findings in a 2008 book called *The State of Native Nations: Conditions under US Policies of Self-Determination.* The studies show that measures of economic development, health, and education tend to be substantially lower for Indigenous groups than for the general population. They are trending upwards, but still suffer from infrastructural impediments, such as chronic federal underfunding and restricted access to services. For example, the average income of an Indigenous person in the United States is about 40 per cent of the national average, and on a per capita basis, health funding for Indigenous people in the United States is significantly lower than that for all other groups receiving federal funding. Studies also show that in most cases, when Indigenous groups gain greater control over economic development, health services, and education, the measures of success and sustainability increase.

Economic and social conditions are generally improving, but it is still common for them to lag significantly behind the general population in both Canada and the United States. A report prepared for the United Nations, *The State of the World's Indigenous Peoples* (Carino et al. 2009), highlights significantly lower life expectancies, incomes, education, and measures of health for the Indigenous populations when compared to the non-Indigenous populations of North America.

The proliferation of Indigenous casinos in the twenty-first century has received considerable attention in recent economic studies; it has also resulted in a fairly new stereotype of the "wealthy Indian," as well as being frequently described as the "new buffalo." While casinos have certainly been a major economic boost for many Indigenous groups, the impact has varied widely. Studies associated with the Harvard Project on American Indian Economic Development showed that real household incomes grew more rapidly in areas without gaming than those with gaming. Many Indigenous groups have rejected gaming for myriad reasons, and many casinos have closed or significantly downsized. As noted by Cattelino (2008), one of the most notable consequences of tribal gaming has been the redistribution of power, money, and media visibility among Indigenous groups.

Many studies show that when Indigenous groups gain more control of economic, health, and educational programs, their success and sustainability improves. However, success and sustainability also depend on having a good Indigenous structure of governance.

NATION-BUILDING

Nation-building involves strengthening the sense of identity among a group of people, often including aspects of self-determination, economic and social development, and cultural pride. Among North American Indigenous peoples, self-determination involves strengthening influence, authority, and claims of sovereignty. Economic development includes initiating and controlling businesses, such as casinos. Social development includes prioritizing programs in health, such as substance abuse and preventable diseases, and programs in education such as with Indigenous-run schools and colleges. Cultural programs include challenging misinformation and stereotypes, taking ownership of traditional knowledge, and maintaining cultural boundaries such as with language, art, and ceremonies.

Nation-building occurs in many ways (see Table 7.1) and on multiple levels. It occurs with individual Indigenous groups (i.e., in each of the

TABLE 7.1
Methods of Nation-Building Used by Indigenous Peoples of North America

- Seeking self-determination and sovereignty
- Gaining control of economic programs
- Gaining control of health and education programs
- Asserting identity (socially, legally, and politically)
- Strengthening influence on local, regional, national, and international levels
- Protecting traditional knowledge
- Resisting cultural appropriation
- Resisting stereotypes and other biases in mainstream culture
- Correcting misinformation
- Developing own education and tourism programs
- Developing own media
- Celebrating culture
- Using anthropologists and anthropological studies in support

more than 1,000 distinct Indigenous First Nations or tribal entities), such as when a group establishes their own economic and social programs; it occurs on regional levels, such as when otherwise independent groups form alliances to enhance program efficiency and celebrate Indigenous identity (e.g., powwows); and it occurs nationally with the advocacy of such groups as the Assembly of First Nations in Canada and the National Congress of American Indians in the United States.

The Role of Anthropology in Nation-Building

There is little doubt that it has been the Indigenous peoples themselves that have taken the initiative for nation-building and have been in control of its growth. There is also little doubt that the growth of Nation-building has been in spite of the challenges and impediments to progress created by non-Indigenous peoples. Indigenous peoples are not averse to using the expertise of others in order to achieve their goals, however, including the work of anthropologists.

Anthropology has had, and continues to have, a significant role in nation-building. Archaeological research and early ethnographies have made significant contributions in support of cultural identity, helping to fill important gaps of knowledge lost through the devastating impacts of colonializaton. As well, information from archaeology and early eth-nographies is often used in support of claims of territory, resources, and sovereignty. This is particularly evident in court cases where the system is generally reluctant to rely on the oral traditions of Indigenous peoples alone. Studies from linguistic anthropology are used to support cultural identity and many linguistic anthropologists work with Indigenous groups to preserve, maintain, and help teach the Indigenous languages. Medical anthropologists are sometimes involved with Indigenous groups in regard to health issues. Many contemporary cultural anthropologists work with Indigenous groups to examine the potential and ongoing impacts of economic and social programs on Indigenous peoples, culture, and communities, such as how an impending project may disrupt their contemporary culture. In this regard, Indigenous groups use anthropological studies to assist them in making informed decisions about whether to resist or to accept projects in or around their lands.

Much of the anthropological work being done in Indigenous communities in the twenty-first century is being done at the request of Indigenous groups. In one sense, since considerable anthropological work is being done with specific goals established by the Indigenous groups that are involved with it, this type of anthropology can be considered applied anthropology.

There also continue to be purely academic anthropology projects (archaeology, cultural anthropology, and linguistics) among Indigenous groups, but it is now common that any "purely academic" project must be also of use to the Indigenous group. This often results in the original research design being modified to meet the needs of both the researcher and the Indigenous group in question.

Protecting Traditional Knowledge

A major issue of concern among Indigenous groups is the protection of Indigenous traditional knowledge. In a report for the United Nations, Carino et al. (2009, 64) state:

> Indigenous traditional knowledge refers to the complex bodies and systems of knowledge, know-how, practices and representations maintained and developed by Indigenous peoples around the world, drawing on a wealth of experience and interaction with the natural environment and transmitted orally from one generation to the next.... Traditional knowledge tends to be collectively owned, whether taking the form of stories, songs, beliefs, customary laws and artwork or scientific, agricultural, technical and ecological knowledge and the skills to implement these technologies and knowledge.

Protecting traditional knowledge has been a primary interest of many North American Indigenous people in recent times and may be considered a form of nation-building. Much of the interest in this area centers on protecting traditional ecological knowledge (TEK).

Traditional ecological knowledge includes an understanding of the lands and resources of an Indigenous group. As outlined by Menzies and Butler (2006), attributes of traditional ecological knowledge include that it is cumulative, dynamic, local, historic, holistic, embedded, and moral and spiritual. Another attribute is that it often documents in **emic** (vs. **etic**) categories. One particular kind of traditional ecological knowledge is that of plant use, such as the medicinal uses of some plants, and many are concerned about protecting such knowledge from being exploited for profit by others.

Who Owns Native Culture?

"Who Owns Native Culture?" is both a major question for Indigenous and non-Indigenous peoples alike; and the title of a seminal book on the intellectual property rights of Indigenous peoples. In the book *Who Owns Native Culture?* anthropologist Michael Brown (2004) outlines how the issue of ownership of Indigenous knowledge and creations emerged in the late twentieth century, at least in part due to a marketplace that turned Indigenous culture into a commodity that could be exploited for commercial purposes. As described by Brown, objections by Indigenous peoples are sometimes economic, insofar as they are rarely compensated for their traditional knowledge and creations that have commercial value; more often, however, objections are based on the loss of control of their own traditions.

Considering the sweat lodge practices common among many Indigenous groups in North America, Brown (2004, 6) writes:

> Some Indians are offended when middle-class Anglo-Americans adopt the sweat lodge ritual as part of their quest for authentic spirituality. Native critics insist that practitioners who fail to observe proper sweat-lodge rules are guilty of blasphemy and cultural aggression. From the perspective of social science, the diffusion of the sweat lodge into Anglo society is threatening to Indians because it blurs the boundaries between native and non-native.

The issue of who owns Native culture is unresolved on many levels. Many Indigenous groups actively work to protect their intellectual property, but the legal system still grapples with identifying ownership of elements of traditional culture. In response, some Indigenous groups have taken to protecting Indigenous knowledge and artistry with trademarks, copyrights, and patents. In Canada, for example, some Indigenous groups have copyrighted prehistoric rock art images. In the United States, the Indian Arts and Crafts Act (1990) seeks to prevent the misrepresentation of arts and crafts

---

BOX 7.1

Mascots, Nicknames, and Logos

The use of sports nicknames, logos, and mascots based on Indigenous peoples of North America is controversial. Many sports teams in the United States and Canada have names that are derived from Indigenous groups, such as "the Indians," "Redskins," "Braves," "Blackhawks," and "Eskimos." Many have Indigenous themed logos and Indigenous themed mascots are common. Supporters of the nicknames, logos, and mascots often claim they are positive representations. Many Indigenous peoples and others, however, claim the nicknames and mascots are demeaning, humiliating, and promote racism, misinformation, and stereotypes. In many people's view, the use of Indigenous-themed mascots, nicknames, and logos are forms of cultural appropriation.

The controversy is centered on college sports teams. In response to complaints and protests, many educational institutions have recently dropped their Indigenous-themed mascots, logos, and nicknames. More than 100 organizations advocate their abolition, including the American Indian Movement, the National Congress of American Indians, some state boards of education, the National Collegiate Athletic Association (NCAA), and the American Anthropological Association.

Guidelines from the NCAA state:

Mascots, nicknames, or images deemed hostile or abusive in terms of race, ethnicity, or national origin should not be visible at championship events controlled by NCAA....

Universities with hostile or abusive mascots, nicknames, or imagery are prohibited from hosting any NCAA championship events....NCAA suggests that institutions follow best practices of institutions that do not support the use of Native American mascots or imagery....

A resolution of the American Anthropological Association states:

We, the members of the American Anthropological Association, call upon all educators and administrators of educational institutions to stop promoting the stereotypical representation of American Indian people through the use of sports mascots. The persistence of such official sanctioned, stereotypical presentations humiliates American Indian people, trivializes the scholarship of anthropologists, undermines the learning environment for all students and seriously compromises efforts to promote diversity on school and college campuses.

---

created by non-Indigenous peoples as authentic. The Indigenous arts and crafts movement in the United States is a billion-dollar industry, and it has been estimated that about 80 per cent of the jewelry and about half of all arts and crafts attributed to Indigenous creativity and manufacture are intentional misrepresentations (Harvard Project 2008).

Cultural Appropriation

A major concern of many Indigenous peoples is the appropriation of Indigenous culture, which occurs in many ways. This includes non-Indigenous people playing Indian in many contexts, ranging from hobbyist movements in Europe to Halloween costumes in North America. It also includes the appropriation of the technology and style of Indigenous arts and crafts,

FIGURE 7.1 No Mascots. Powwow participant displaying an anti-mascot pin. (Photo © Getty Images / Mike Simons. Reprinted by permission.)

as well as the appropriation of images. Indigenous images are often used by both businesses and governments for promotion. **Cigar store Indians**, for example, have a long history of use in the United States to draw people into stores; **inuksuks** are now widely appropriated by non-Indigenous groups in Canada; and images of Indigenous peoples, places, and things are commonly used throughout the continent to promote tourism by non-Indigenous governments and businesses.

Mascots, nicknames, and logos for sports teams are other major areas of concern (see Box 7.1), as is the use of Indigenous labels for selling commercial products. Many names of vehicles, for example—such as the Pontiac, Jeep Cherokee, and Winnebago—are all derived from Indigenous groups. Critics argue that the use of Indigenous images, names, and other aspects of culture tend to be derogatory and perpetuate stereotypical images. Critics also question why many non-Indigenous people think it is acceptable to use mascots, names, and logos derived from Indigenous groups for sports teams and commercial products in spite of the protests of the Indigenous peoples, and despite the fact that it is no longer acceptable to do the same for African American, Latino, and other minority or ethnic groups in North America or elsewhere.

Asserting Identity

Asserting identity, in both individual and group contexts, is an important component of nation-building. In the twenty-first century, Indigenous peoples of North America continue to exert their identity in multiple ways. In many instances, the assertions are political and confrontational. In most cases, however, the assertions of identity are much more subtle, such as taking control of terminology. The descriptor "First Nations," widely used in Canada, was initiated largely by the Indigenous peoples who live there. Increasingly, Indigenous peoples refer to themselves as a member of a particular nation or tribe, and in many public forums Indigenous peoples have begun speaking with words from their own languages. Another way identity is now commonly asserted is through the increasing use of traditional ceremonial dress in public ceremonies.

Regaining Control

There are many ways in which Indigenous groups are maintaining or regaining control of their cultures. Some Indigenous groups have established their own permit system for researchers working in their territories. For archaeological work, for example, this now means that an archaeologist must get a permit from the federal, state, or provincial government as well as from the Indigenous group that has claims on the land in question.

Many groups have been developing their own education programs, both for their own members as well as for public education. Archaeologists, cultural anthropologists, and linguists are often involved in the creation of these programs.

The repatriation of artifacts and human remains from museums and other institutions is another way of regaining control. Repatriated artifacts are commonly curated in museums or other repositories created and maintained by the Indigenous groups. Repatriated human remains are often reburied or cremated. In addition to creating and controlling their own museums or repositories, many Indigenous groups work in collaboration or partnership with existing museums to ensure an authentic or otherwise culturally acceptable portrayal of their cultures. The National Museum of the American Indian, located in Washington, DC, for example, employs Indigenous researchers and curators.

Many Indigenous groups now develop their own cultural tourism programs, including heritage parks (often archaeological sites and/or reconstructed villages), as well as tours through their traditional territories. In addition to having an economic impact, such programs usually provide authentic Indigenous interpretation for tourists. Programs are often based on the work of early ethnographers and archaeological research. Anthropologists are also often involved in the creation and maintenance of these programs.

Another way of ensuring control over how Indigenous cultures are portrayed is through contracts with researchers. It is now common for anthropologists and other researchers working with Indigenous groups to sign contracts with clauses outlining the ownership and dissemination of information accumulated during their studies. Some Indigenous groups have also developed their own book-publishing programs.

Righting Past Wrongs

Addressing past wrongs may be viewed as an important stage of reconciliation and nation-building. To this end, the governments of both Canada and the United States are increasingly recognizing and accepting responsibility for the harm they have done to Indigenous peoples and their cultures. In 1998, for example, the Canadian government issued an apology that read:

> The government of Canada today formally expresses to all Aboriginal People in Canada our profound regret for past actions of the federal government which have contributed to these difficult pages in the history of our relationships together.

This apology followed the report on the Royal Commission on Aboriginal Peoples. Members of the commission included both Indigenous and non-Indigenous peoples, and the report was based on public hearings, commissioned research studies by anthropologists and other social scientists, and consultation with experts. The central conclusion of the 4,000-page report was that "The main policy directly pursued for more than 150 years, first by colonial then by Canadian governments, has been wrong."

Governments have continued to offer apologies since then. Appendix 5, for example, provides the text of a 2008 apology to the Aboriginal Peoples of Canada for subjecting them to residential schools, and Appendix 6 provides the text of a 2009 apology to Native Americans.

Besides apologies, the wrongs that have been inflicted upon Indigenous peoples of the entire continent are being addressed in the twenty-first century in multiple other ways. Many of the methods begun in the historical period, such as protests, confrontation, litigation, and negotiation, still continue, though protests and confrontations are not as prominent as they were in earlier times. Many claims of wrongdoings are settled in courts, and others through negotiation with governments.

CONTEMPORARY ANTHROPOLOGY WITH INDIGENOUS COMMUNITIES

Anthropology continues to have an important role in many Indigenous communities. In many ways, however, Indigenous peoples have changed the nature of why and how anthropological research is done and reported. In the early twenty-first century, Indigenous groups have considerable control over anthropological research.

Archaeological projects are often done at the request of Indigenous groups, and when they aren't, the archaeologists often consult with the group before beginning their work. As well, Indigenous groups often request linguists to assist with the preservation of their language. Much of the collaborative work between Indigenous groups and archaeologists and linguists may be considered applied anthropology.

In some instances, ethnography may be requested by an Indigenous group; this may be considered applied anthropology, but considerable ethnographic research is still primarily academic in nature. Ethnography in recent and contemporary times is considerably different than the ethnography that was undertaken from the mid-1800s until the late 1900s. At that time, ethnography was primarily descriptive and largely attempted to provide broad overviews of multiple aspects of culture, such as social systems, political systems, and ideology. Table 7.2 lists the characteristics of ethnographic research undertaken by ethnographers collaborating with Indigenous groups in North America in recent and contemporary times.

Most of the characteristics of contemporary ethnography listed in Table 7.2 require little explanation. However, the last point—that ethnographies are now often explicitly situated in theory—may be an exception. Traditionally, theory frames the ethnographic work. One common theoretical framework is that of "**frontier theory**." What this means is that the anthropology is framed with the understanding that the recent history of Indigenous peoples in North America has been played out against a backdrop of Europeans and their descendants: (i) occupying the traditional lands of the Indigenous peoples with the understanding that they had a right to do so; (ii) believing that the land's resources were free for the taking; and (iii) believing that Indigenous people were intellectually inferior. In many parts of North America, contemporary relations between Indigenous and non-Indigenous peoples remain framed within this frontier mentality.

There are many other theoretical frameworks to work with, such as those related to language, identity, gender, politics, revitalization, and more. These frameworks are in some ways a reflection of the changing interests in ethnographic research, both for anthropologists and for Indig-

TABLE 7.2

Characteristics of Ethnographic Research Undertaken among Indigenous Groups of North America in Recent and Contemporary Times

---

Research is undertaken for a variety of reasons (applied and academic)

Research is largely under the control of Indigenous administration (e.g., tribal governments)

Focus of research is often determined by the Indigenous group

Although traditional participant-observation continues in some communities, considerable research now occurs in non-traditional places, such as schools and casinos

Popular foci include traditional ecological knowledge, traditional use, identity, language, revitalization, spirituality, politics, education, and law

Research focuses on contemporary culture

Ethnographies often reflective (e.g., anthropologist explicitly reflects on her or his role and impact in the community)

Ethnographies often include an explicit recognition of the anthropologist's bias (e.g., age, gender)

Ethnographies often written in a narrative style (e.g., like a story, with the anthropologist included)

Ethnographies often provide an Indigenous voice (e.g., providing the etic perspective of the Indigenous people as well as the etic perspective of the anthropologist)

Ethnographies usually explicitly situated in theory (e.g., frontier theory, revitalization theory)

---

enous groups. Reviewing recent ethnographic information on North American Indigenous peoples, Pauline Turner Strong (2005, 256) writes:

> The hallmark of traditional ethnographic research has been intensive, long-term participant-observation in a local community. This remains a significant mode of research, although today participant observation often takes place in institutional settings such as tribal schools, museums, cultural centers, casinos, and tourist complexes.... This shift is due in part to indigenous preferences: These institutions have come to serve as mediators between indigenous communities and the outside world, and they are sites in which scholars can contribute to community-based research without intruding on private life. At the same time, such institutions are ideal for the study of processes of self-representation, self-determination, repatriation, and economic development....

The demographic make-up of those who practice anthropology has also changed in recent years. Orin Starn (2011, 184–85) writes:

> ... in the last decade or so, the anthropology of Native America has seen something of a re-birth, albeit in ways almost unrecognizable from the days of Boas and Kroeber. Perhaps the most obvious change has come in

demographics of who studies Native America. Along with other transformations, recent decades have witnessed anthropology's regendering from a mostly male to a mainly female profession.... More people of color and from the Third World have also entered into the profession's ranks, partly unsettling the old colonial calculus where white people always did the studying and brown people were always the studied. In line with these disciplinary developments, a predominantly female new generation of Native American scholars is increasingly shaping the anthropology of Native America.

BATTLING MISUNDERSTANDINGS

Battling misunderstandings and unfounded stereotypes about the Indigenous peoples of North America has long been a focus of interest among both Indigenous groups and those anthropologists who study them. There have been numerous scholarly books and articles in academic journals and Indigenous media focusing on these battles. The audience, however, has been limited, and in many ways those articles have been preaching to the converted.

In recent times, however, books with a wider appeal—especially to non-academic or general audiences—have begun to emerge, bringing the issues of misunderstanding and unfounded stereotypes to the public. Recent, popular books with the goal of correcting information include those by both Indigenous scholars and anthropologists. For example, the book *Everything You Know about Indians is Wrong* (2009) is written for a general audience. Author and Indigenous (Comanche) scholar Paul Chaat Smith debunks many misconceptions about the history and culture of the Indigenous peoples of North America. Examples include revealing the inauthenticity of the well-known Chief Seattle speech in the 1800s (which Smith exposes as having been rewritten to reflect ideas of the environmental movement in the 1970s); a popular and best-selling autobiography purportedly of an Indigenous person that turns out to be fiction written by a non-Indigenous person; and the many incorrect, stereotypical Hollywood portrayals of the Indigenous peoples of North America, including those in popular movies such as *Dances with Wolves*, *Last of the Mohicans*, and *Geronimo*. Smith's book is one of many that have appeared in recent years that are critical of the stereotypes portrayed in Hollywood movies. In regards to the popular view of all North American Indians being that of a mid-nineteenth century person from a Plains tribe, Smith states (2009, 20), "Most Indians weren't anything like the Sioux or Comanche, either the real ones or the Hollywood invention."

Anthropologists are also beginning to publish on this issue outside of scholarly publications. Anthropologist John Steckley, for example, wrote *White Lies about the Inuit* (2008) to specifically address the misinformation about Inuit people and culture that is perpetuated not only in popular culture, but in textbooks as well. He covers several popular misconceptions about the Inuit, including wife-sharing, rubbing noses, Arctic hysteria, and the number of words for snow. In regards to the widespread belief that in times of stress, elders are sometimes abandoned on ice floes in a kind of assisted suicide, Steckley (2008, 106) writes, "Calling Inuit elder suicide a culturally mandated practice is like saying that husbands and fathers in Toronto are culturally mandated to commit family murder-suicide when they feel economic or personal failure. Sure it happens, but it does not reflect cultural custom."

One of the most important misunderstandings among the general, non-Indigenous population is the popular perception of what defines Indigenous (or Indian, or Aboriginal, etc.) identity. As mentioned in Chapter 1, Indian identity is complex and membership criteria vary widely among the more than 1,000 distinct tribal entities and First Nations in the United States and Canada. Even beyond knowing these criteria, however, there often remains an underlying (and sometimes not-so-underlying) subtext among some people that when Indigenous peoples have adopted non-Indigenous cultural traits, they have in a sense given up their "Indianness." For many Indigenous people and anthropologists, this view is nonsense. As mentioned in Chapter 2, cultures continually change. One can still be Indigenous and have Indigenous culture while adopting cultural traits from others.

Thomas McIlwraith (2012) relates a story of his own ethnographic work with a group for whom hunting remains a key part of their culture. In the story, McIlwraith describes an elder's explanation of how hunting in the past was done by walking and with the assistance of dogs, and how today they hunt with vehicles. In the end, though, the elder indicated that the group was still Native even though they now used vehicles. Anthropologists understand this, but unfortunately many others don't.

Similarly, anthropologists understand how Indigenous peoples can use cell phones and have powwows in modern structures (see Figure 1.3), drive vehicles, use rifles, and eat pizza, all the while retaining their Indigenous identities. Convincing those who remain locked in their notions that "Indian cultures" are static is one of the greatest hurdles facing Indigenous peoples and anthropologists today. As noted by anthropologist Wayne Warry (2008), understanding the differences between a view of culture as static and a view of culture as fluid is an important step to take in understanding Indigenous peoples.

FIGURE 7.2 Native Americans with Capitol. Native Americans maintaining their culture and identity during a powwow at the National Mall in Washington, DC. (Photo © Smithsonian Institute Archives. Image # 2002–15248.)

CONTEMPORARY CONDITIONS, NATION-BUILDING, AND ANTHROPOLOGY IN A GLOBAL PERSPECTIVE

Indigenous peoples around the world tend to have lower measures of economic prosperity, health, and education than the non-Indigenous peoples living in the same countries. The Indigenous peoples in North America share these traits with other Indigenous groups globally.

Nation-building among Indigenous peoples has varying rates of success. In many countries—especially in Asia and Africa—the Indigenous peoples have had much less success with nation-building. As they do in many other respects, the Indigenous peoples of North America have the closest similarity with the Indigenous peoples of Australia and New Zealand in terms of their nation-building efforts, which is understandable given their similar colonial and post-colonial histories. These histories include similar associations between Indigenous groups and anthropologists, with anthropologists largely playing supportive roles in Indigenous nation-building.

SUGGESTED READINGS

For overviews of the economic and social conditions of Indigenous peoples of the United States, *The State of Native Nations: Conditions under US Policies of Self-Determination* by the Harvard Project on American Indian

Economic Development (2008) is a good source. For Indigenous groups in Canada, the *Report of the Royal Commission on Aboriginal Peoples* (1996) is recommended.

The State of the World's Indigenous Populations by Carino et al. (2009) includes data on the social and economic welfare of Indigenous groups in both Canada and the Unites States. It is a good source for specific information in those countries—and, since it provides data from many other countries as well, it is an excellent source for global comparisons.

There is extensive literature on the use of Indigenous mascots and nicknames for sports teams. *The Native American Mascot Controversy: A Handbook*, edited by C. Richard King (2010), brings together dozens of articles, essays, commentaries, policies, resolutions, and legislation on the subject.

Regarding the appropriation of Indigenous culture, *Who Owns Native Culture?* by Michael Brown (2004) and *Playing Indian* by Philip Deloria (1998) are both highly recommended.

Suggestions for general reading on stereotypes include *The White Man's Indian* by Robert F. Berkhofer, Jr. (1978); *The Imaginary Indian* by Daniel Francis (1992); and *Dressing in Feathers: The Construction of the Indian in American Popular Culture*, edited by S. Elizabeth Bird (1996). For specific focus on the portrayal of North American Indigenous peoples in movies, books by Buscombe (2006), Kilpatrick (1999), and Rollins and O'Connor (1998) are recommended. A good source on news media bias regarding Indigenous peoples of North America is *Native Americans in the News* by Weston (1996).

Some recent ethnographic studies reflecting the characteristics of contemporary ethnology include *Maps and Dreams* by Hugh Brody (2004); *Wisdom Sits in Places* by Keith Basso (1996); *Critical Inuit Studies: An Anthology of Contemporary Arctic Ethnography*, edited by Pamela Stern and Lisa Stevenson (2006); and *"We Are Still Didene": Stories of Hunting and History from Northern British Columbia* by Thomas McIlwraith (2012).

Spirits of Our Whaling Ancestors: Revitalizing Makah and Nuu-chah-nulth Traditions by Charlotte Cote (2010) is an excellent example of contemporary anthropological scholarship. Cote, a professor of American Indian Studies and a member of the Nuu-chah-nulth Nation, examines a return to whale hunting among some Northwest Coast groups in the contexts of revitalization, identity, and self-determination.

Overviews of recent trends in the anthropology of Indigenous peoples of North America are provided by Pauline Turner Strong (2005) and Jessica Cattelino (2010).

FINAL COMMENTS

Books such as this are meant to do many things, including providing basic information on both the Indigenous peoples of North America and anthropology. Even though this book is concise, there is still a lot of information in it.

My hope is that while readers obtain a sense of the Indigenous peoples of North America from an anthropological perspective, they also appreciate that this book has barely touched the surface. Much has been sacrificed in the interests of brevity. One of the risks of depending on a concise book such as this is that it is difficult to convey the diversity of cultures, interests, and issues of the Indigenous peoples and anthropology.

I suspect that most readers of this book have read it primarily for the information about Indigenous peoples. For those people, I hope that they have come to understand at least a bit about anthropology as well.

Similarly, for the readers that have read the book primarily for the anthropology, I hope that they have come to appreciate the past and present situations of the Indigenous peoples of North America.

The book has essentially been written based on tens of thousands of pages from hundreds of scholarly articles, books, and reports, enhanced by my own experiences teaching and working with Indigenous peoples in the framework of anthropology. It has been pared down to be concise. However, there is still a lot to remember, and it is unreasonable to think that most of what is in this book will be retained.

Accordingly, below is a list of what I consider to be most essential. This is the basic information that I hope all readers will be able to retain for many years to come, without having to resort to looking it up. I also hope that this information will be passed on to others.

1. *There are many different labels for the Indigenous peoples of North America, each with its own meaning.* "Indigenous" is an umbrella term for all people who can trace ancestry to the peoples who lived in North America before the arrival of Europeans about 500 years ago, but other terms such as "Indian" and "Aboriginal" retain specific meanings.
2. *The archaeological record of prehistoric North America is vast.* There are hundreds of thousands of archaeological sites and millions of artifacts used to document the activities of the ancestors of contemporary Indigenous peoples in North America.
3. *Prior to the arrival of Europeans, North America was populated by a wide variety of peoples and cultures.* There were millions of people speaking hundreds of different languages; the diversity of economic, social, political, and ideological systems was enormous.
4. *The colonialization of the continent by Europeans was devastating to Indigenous peoples and cultures.* Population loss was severe and there was an almost total disruption of traditional lifeways.
5. *Indigenous peoples have been remarkably resilient.* Despite centuries of colonialization, with government policies and practices deliberately designed to obliterate Indigenous culture, it remains strong; and research suggests that when Indigenous peoples gain increasing control of economic and social programs, there is a greater chance for their success.
6. *The development of North American anthropology has been intricately intertwined with the Indigenous peoples of the continent.* Anthropology continues to have an important role in Indigenous communities, and is often undertaken at the request of, or in collaboration with, Indigenous peoples.

Those interested in pursuing further research on the Indigenous peoples of North America are directed to the suggested readings at the end of each chapter, and to "Appendix 7: Studying the Indigenous Peoples of North America."

THE UNITED NATIONS DECLARATION ON THE RIGHTS OF INDIGENOUS PEOPLES

Following are all of the articles of the declaration, adopted by the General Assembly in 2007. The full Declaration, including the lengthy preamble, can be found on the website of the United Nations Permanent Forum on Indigenous issues: www.un.org/esa/socdev/unpfii/en/declaration.html.

Article 1   Indigenous peoples have the right to the full enjoyment, as a collective or as individuals, of all human rights and fundamental freedoms as recognized in the Charter of the United Nations, the Universal Declaration of Human Rights, and international human rights law.

Article 2   Indigenous peoples and individuals are free and equal to all other peoples and individuals and have the right to be free from any kind of discrimination, in the exercise of their rights, in particular that based on their indigenous origin or identity.

Article 3   Indigenous peoples have the right to self-determination. By virtue of that right they freely determine their political status and freely pursue their economic, social and cultural development.

Article 4   Indigenous peoples, in exercising their right to self-determination, have the right to autonomy or self-government in matters relating to their internal and local affairs, as well as ways and means for financing their autonomous functions.

Article 5   Indigenous peoples have the right to maintain and strengthen their distinct political, legal, economic, social and cultural institutions, while retaining their right to participate fully, if they so choose, in the political, economic, social and cultural life of the State.

Article 6   Every indigenous individual has the right to a nationality.

Article 7   1. Indigenous individuals have the rights to life, physical and mental integrity, liberty and security of person.

2. Indigenous peoples have the collective right to live in freedom, peace and security as distinct peoples and shall not be subjected to any act of genocide or any other act of violence, including forcibly removing children of the group to another group.

Article 8   1. Indigenous peoples and individuals have the right not to be subjected to forced assimilation or destruction of their culture.

2. States shall provide effective mechanism for prevention of, and redress for:

(a) Any action which has the aim or effect of depriving them of their integrity as distinct peoples, or of their cultural values or ethnic identities;

(b) Any action which has the aim or effect of dispossessing them of their lands, territories or resources;

(c) Any form of forced population transfer which has the aim or effect of violating or undermining any of their rights;

(d) Any form of forced assimilation or integration;

(e) Any form of propaganda designed to promote or incite racial or ethnic discrimination directed against them.

Article 9   Indigenous peoples and individuals have the right to belong to an indigenous community or nation, in accordance with the traditions and customs of the community or nation concerned. No discrimination of any kind may arise from the exercise of such a right.

Article 10   Indigenous peoples shall not be forcibly removed from their lands or territories. No relocation shall take place without the free, prior and informed consent of the indigenous peoples concerned and after agreement on just and fair compensation and, where possible, with the option of return.

Article 11   1. Indigenous peoples have the right to practise and revitalize their cultural traditions and customs. This includes the right to maintain, protect and develop the past, present and future manifestations of their cultures, such as archaeological and historical sites, artefacts, designs, ceremonies, technologies and visual and performing arts and literature.

2. States shall provide redress through effective mechanisms, which may include restitution, developed in conjunction with indigenous peoples, with respect to their cultural, intellectual, religious and spiritual property taken without their free, prior and informed consent or in violation of their laws, traditions and customs.

Article 12   1. Indigenous peoples have the right to manifest, practise, develop and teach their spiritual and religious traditions, customs and ceremonies; the right to maintain, protect, and have access in privacy to their religious and cultural sites; the right to the use and control of their ceremonial objects; and the right to the repatriation of their human remains.

2. States shall seek to enable the access and/or repatriation of ceremonial objects and human remains in their possession through fair, transparent and effective mechanisms developed in conjunction with indigenous peoples concerned.

Article 13   1. Indigenous peoples have the right to revitalize, use, develop and transmit to future generations their histories, languages, oral traditions, philosophies, writing systems and literatures, and to designate and retain their own names for communities, places and persons.

2. States shall take effective measures to ensure that this right is protected and also to ensure that indigenous peoples can understand and be understood in political, legal and administrative proceedings, where necessary through the provision of interpretation or by other appropriate means.

Article 14   1. Indigenous peoples have the right to establish and control their educational systems and institutions providing education in their own languages, in a manner appropriate to their cultural methods of teaching and learning.

2. Indigenous individuals, particularly children, have the right to all levels and forms of education of the State without discrimination.

3. States shall, in conjunction with indigenous peoples, take effective measures, in order for indigenous individuals, particularly children, including those living outside their communities, to have access, when possible, to an education in their own culture and provided in their own language.

Article 15   1. Indigenous peoples have the right to the dignity and diversity of their cultures, traditions, histories and aspirations which shall be appropriately reflected in education and public information.

2. States shall take effective measures, in consultation and cooperation with the indigenous peoples concerned, to combat prejudice and eliminate discrimination and to promote tolerance, understanding and good relations among indigenous peoples and all other segments of society.

Article 16   1. Indigenous peoples have the right to establish their own media in their own languages and to have access to all forms of non-indigenous media without discrimination.

2. States shall take effective measures to ensure that State-owned media duly reflect indigenous cultural diversity. States, without prejudice to ensuring full freedom of expression, should encourage privately owned media to adequately reflect indigenous cultural diversity.

Article 17   1. Indigenous individuals and peoples have the right to enjoy fully all rights established under applicable international and domestic labour law.

2. States shall in consultation and cooperation with indigenous peoples take specific measures to protect indigenous children from economic exploitation and from performing any work that is likely to be hazardous or to interfere with the child's education, or to be harmful to the child's health or physical, mental, spiritual, moral or social development, taking into account their special vulnerability and the importance of education for their empowerment.

3. Indigenous individuals have the right not to be subjected to any discriminatory conditions of labour and, inter alia, employment or salary.

Article 18   Indigenous peoples have the right to participate in decision-making in matters which would affect their rights, through representatives chosen by themselves in accordance with their own procedures, as well as to maintain and develop their own indigenous decision-making institutions.

Article 19   States shall consult and cooperate in good faith with the indigenous peoples concerned through their own representative institutions in order to obtain their free, prior and informed consent before adopting and implementing legislative or administrative measures that may affect them.

Article 20 1. Indigenous peoples have the right to maintain and develop their political, economic and social systems or institutions, to be secure in the enjoyment of their own means of subsistence and development, and to engage freely in all their traditional and other economic activities.

2. Indigenous peoples deprived of their means of subsistence and development are entitled to just and fair redress.

Article 21 1. Indigenous peoples have the right, without discrimination, to the improvement of their economic and social conditions, including, inter alia, in the areas of education, employment, vocational training and retraining, housing, sanitation, health and social security.

2. States shall take effective measures and, where appropriate, special measures to ensure continuing improvement of their economic and social conditions. Particular attention shall be paid to the rights and special needs of indigenous elders, women, youth, children and persons with disabilities.

Article 22 1. Particular attention shall be paid to the rights and special needs of indigenous elders, women, youth, children and persons with disabilities in the implementation of this Declaration.

2. States shall take measures, in conjunction with indigenous peoples, to ensure that indigenous women and children enjoy the full protection and guarantees against all forms of violence and discrimination.

Article 23 Indigenous peoples have the right to determine and develop priorities and strategies for exercising their right to development. In particular, indigenous peoples have the right to be actively involved in developing and determining health, housing and other economic and social programmes affecting them and, as far as possible, to administer such programmes through their own institutions.

Article 24 1. Indigenous peoples have the right to their traditional medicines and to maintain their health practices, including the conservation of their vital medicinal plants, animals and minerals. Indigenous individuals also have the right to access, without any discrimination, to all social and health services.

2. Indigenous individuals have an equal right to the enjoyment of the highest attainable standard of physical and mental health. States shall take the necessary steps with a view to achieving progressively the full realization of this right.

Article 25 Indigenous peoples have the right to maintain and strengthen their distinctive spiritual relationship with their traditionally owned or otherwise occupied and used lands, territories, waters and coastal seas and other resources and to uphold their responsibilities to future generations in this regard.

Article 26 1. Indigenous peoples have the right to the lands, territories and resources which they have traditionally owned, occupied or otherwise used or acquired.

2. Indigenous peoples have the right to own, use, develop and control the lands, territories and resources that they possess by reason of traditional ownership or other traditional occupation or use, as well as those which they have otherwise acquired.

3. States shall give legal recognition and protection to these lands, territories and resources. Such recognition shall be conducted with due respect to the customs, traditions and land tenure systems of the indigenous peoples concerned.

Article 27 States shall establish and implement, in conjunction with indigenous peoples concerned, a fair, independent, impartial, open and transparent process, giving due recognition to indigenous peoples' laws, traditions, customs and land tenure systems, to recognize and adjudicate the rights of indigenous peoples pertaining to their lands, territories and resources, including those which were traditionally owned or otherwise occupied or used. Indigenous peoples shall have the right to participate in this process.

Article 28 1. Indigenous peoples have the right to redress, by means that can include restitution or, when this not possible, just, fair and equitable compensation, for the lands, territories and resources which they have traditionally owned or otherwise occupied or used, and which have been confiscated, taken, occupied, used, or damaged without their free, prior and informed consent.

2. Unless otherwise freely agreed upon by the peoples concerned, compensation shall take the form of lands, territories and resources equal in quality, size and legal status or of monetary compensation or other appropriate redress.

Article 29 1. Indigenous peoples have the right to the conservation and protection of the environment and the productive capacity of their lands or territories and resources. States shall establish and implement assistance programmes for indigenous peoples for such conservation and protection, without discrimination.

2. States shall take effective measures to ensure that no storage or disposal of hazardous materials shall take place in the lands or territories of indigenous peoples without their free, prior and informed consent.

3. States shall also take effective measures to ensure, as needed, that programmes for monitoring, maintaining and restoring the health of indigenous peoples, as developed and implemented by the peoples affected by such materials, are duly implemented.

Article 30   1. Military activities shall not take place in the lands or territories of indigenous peoples, unless justified by a relevant public interest or otherwise freely agreed with or requested by the indigenous peoples concerned.

2. States shall undertake effective consultations with the indigenous peoples concerned, through appropriate procedures and in particular through their representative institutions, prior to using their lands or territories for military activities.

Article 31   1. Indigenous peoples have the right to maintain, control, protect and develop their cultural heritage, traditional knowledge and traditional cultural expressions, as well as the manifestations of their sciences, technologies and cultures, including human and genetic resources, seeds, medicines, knowledge of the properties of fauna and flora, oral traditions, literatures, designs, sports and traditional games and visual and performing arts. They also have the right to maintain, control, protect and develop their intellectual property over such cultural heritage, traditional knowledge, and traditional cultural expressions.

2. In conjunction with indigenous peoples, States shall take effective measures to recognize and protect the exercise of these rights.

Article 32   1. Indigenous peoples have the right to determine and develop priorities and strategies for the development or use of their lands or territories and other resources.

2. States shall consult and cooperate in good faith with the indigenous peoples concerned through their own representative institutions in order to obtain their free and informed consent prior to the approval of any project affecting their lands or territories and other resources, particularly in connection with the development, utilization or exploitation of mineral, water, or other resources.

3. States shall provide effective mechanisms for just and fair redress for

any such activities, and appropriate measures shall be taken to mitigate adverse environmental, economic, social, cultural or spiritual impact.

Article 33   1. Indigenous peoples have the right to determine their own identity or membership in accordance with their customs and traditions. This does not impair the right of indigenous individuals to obtain citizenship of the States in which they live.

2. Indigenous peoples have the right to determine the structures and to select the membership of their institutions in accordance with their own procedures.

Article 34   Indigenous peoples have the right to promote, develop and maintain their institutional structures and their distinctive customs, spirituality, traditions, procedures, practices and, in the cases where they exist, juridical systems or customs, in accordance with international human rights standards.

Article 35   Indigenous peoples have the right to determine the responsibilities of individuals to their communities.

Article 36   1. Indigenous peoples, in particular those divided by international borders, have the right to maintain and develop contacts, relations and cooperation, including activities for spiritual, cultural, political, economic and social purposes, with their own members as well as other peoples across borders.

2. States, in consultation and cooperation with indigenous peoples, shall take effective measures to facilitate the exercise and ensure the implementation of this right.

Article 37   1. Indigenous peoples have the right to the recognition, observance and enforcement of treaties, agreements and other constructive arrangements concluded with States or their successors and to have States honour and respect such treaties, agreements and other constructive arrangements.

2. Nothing in this Declaration may be interpreted as diminishing or eliminating the rights of indigenous peoples contained in treaties, agreements and other constructive arrangements.

Article 38   States, in consultation and cooperation with indigenous peoples, shall take the appropriate measures, including legislative measures, to achieve the ends of this Declaration.

Article 39   Indigenous peoples have the right to have access to financial and technical assistance from States and through international cooperation, for the enjoyment of the rights contained in this Declaration.

Article 40   Indigenous peoples have the right to access to and prompt decision through just and fair procedures for the resolution of conflicts and disputes with States or other parties, as well as to effective remedies for all infringements of their individual and collective rights. Such a decision shall give due consideration to the customs, traditions, rules and legal systems of the indigenous peoples concerned and international human rights.

Article 41   The organs and specialized agencies of the United Nations system and other intergovernmental organizations shall contribute to the full realization of the provisions of this Declaration through the mobilization, inter alia, of financial cooperation and technical assistance. Ways and means of ensuring participation of indigenous peoples on issues affecting them shall be established.

Article 42   The United Nations, its bodies, including the Permanent Forum on Indigenous Issues, and specialized agencies, including at the country level, and States shall promote respect for and full application of the provisions of this Declaration and followup the effectiveness of this Declaration.

Article 43   The rights recognized herein constitute the minimum standards for the survival, dignity and well-being of the indigenous peoples of the world.

Article 44   All the rights and freedoms recognized herein are equally guaranteed to male and female indigenous individuals.

Article 45   Nothing in this Declaration may be construed as diminishing or extinguishing the rights indigenous peoples have now or may acquire in the future.

Article 46   1. Nothing in this Declaration may be interpreted as implying for any State, people, group or person any right to engage in any activity or to perform any act contrary to the Charter of the United Nations or construed as authorizing or encouraging any action which would dismember or impair, totally or in part, the territorial integrity or political unity of sovereign and independent States.

2. In the exercise of the rights enunciated in the present Declaration, human rights and fundamental freedoms of all shall be respected. The exercise of the rights set forth in this Declaration shall be subject only to such limitations as are determined by law and in accordance with international human rights obligations. Any such limitations shall be non-discriminatory and strictly necessary solely for the purpose of securing due recognition and respect for the rights and freedoms of others and for meeting the just and most compelling requirements of a democratic society.

3. The provisions set forth in this Declaration shall be interpreted in accordance with the principles of justice, democracy, respect for human rights, equality, non-discrimination, good governance and good faith.

EXCERPTS FROM THE CODE OF ETHICS OF THE AMERICAN ANTHROPOLOGICAL ASSOCIATION (2009)

... In both proposing and carrying out research, anthropological researchers must be open about the purpose(s), potential impacts, and source(s) of support for research projects with funders, colleagues, persons studied or providing information, and with relevant parties affected by the research....

A1 Anthropological researchers have primary ethical obligations to the people, species, and materials they study and to the people with whom they work. These obligations can supersede the goal of seeking new knowledge....
These ethical obligations include:
- To avoid harm or wrong, understanding that the development of knowledge can lead to change which may be positive or negative for the people or animals worked with or studied....

2 In conducting and publishing their research, or otherwise disseminating their research results, anthropological researchers must ensure that they do not harm the safety, dignity, or privacy of the people with whom they work, conduct research, or perform other professional activities, or who might reasonably be thought to be affected by their research....

4 Anthropological researchers should obtain in advance the informed consent of persons being studied, providing information, owning or

controlling access to material being studied, or otherwise identified as having interests which might be impacted by the research....

6   While anthropologists may gain personally from their work, they must not exploit individuals, groups, animals, or cultural or biological materials. They should recognize their debt to the societies in which they work and their obligation to reciprocate with people studied in appropriate ways....

B4 Anthropologists should never deceive the people they are studying regarding the sponsorship, goals, methods, products, or expected impacts of their work....

EXCERPTS FROM THE NATIVE AMERICAN GRAVES PROTECTION AND REPATRIATION ACT (1990)

The complete Native American Graves Protection and Repatriation Act can be found on the website of the United States National Park Service, US Department of the Interior: www.nps.gov/history/nagpra.

SECTION 3. OWNERSHIP.

(A) Native American Human Remains and Objects.

The ownership or control of Native American cultural items which are excavated or discovered on Federal or tribal lands after November 16, 1990, shall be (with priority given in the order listed)—

(1) in the case of Native American human remains and associated funerary objects, in the lineal descendants of the Native American; or

(2) in any case in which such lineal descendants cannot be ascertained, and in the case of unassociated funerary objects, sacred objects, and objects of cultural patrimony—

(A) in the Indian tribe or Native Hawaiian organization on whose tribal land such objects or remains were discovered;

(B) in the Indian tribe or Native Hawaiian organization which has the closest cultural affiliation with such remains or objects and which, upon notice, states a claim for such remains or objects; or

(C) if the cultural affiliation of the objects cannot be reasonably ascertained and if the objects were discovered on Federal land that is recognized by a final judgement of the Indian Claims Commission or the United States Court of Claims as the aboriginal land of some Indian tribe—

(1) [sic] in the Indian tribe that is recognized as aboriginally occupying the area in which the objects were discovered, if upon notice, such tribe states a claim for such remains or objects, or

(2) [sic] if it can be shown by a preponderance of the evidence that a different tribe has a stronger cultural relationship with the remains or objects than the tribe or organization specified in paragraph (1), in the Indian tribe that has the strongest demonstrated relationship, if upon notice, such tribe states a claim for such remains or objects....

SECTION 5. INVENTORY FOR HUMAN REMAINS AND ASSOCIATED FUNERARY OBJECTS.

(A) In General.
Each Federal agency and each museum which has possession or control over holdings or collections of Native American human remains and associated funerary objects shall compile an inventory of such items and, to the extent possible based on information possessed by such museum or Federal agency, identify the geographical and cultural affiliation of such item....

SECTION 7. REPATRIATION.

(A) Repatriation of Native American Human Remains and Objects Possessed or Controlled by Federal Agencies and Museums.
(1) If, pursuant to section 5 of this act [25 U.S.C. 3003], the cultural affiliation of Native American human remains and associated funerary objects with a particular Indian tribe or Native Hawaiian organization is established, then the Federal agency or museum, upon the request of a known lineal descendant of the Native American or of the tribe or organization and pursuant to subsections (b) and (e) of this section, shall expeditiously return such remains and associated funerary objects....

EXCERPTS FROM THE ROYAL PROCLAMATION OF 1763

By the King, a Royal Proclamation

Whereas We have taken into Our Royal Consideration the extensive and valuable Acquisitions in America, secured to Our Crown ... We have thought fit, with the Advice of our Privy Council, to issue this our Royal Proclamation....

And whereas it is just and reasonable, and essential to our interest, and the Security of our Colonies, that the several Nations or Tribes of Indians with whom We are connected, and who live under our Protection, should not be molested or disturbed in the Possession of such Parts of Our Dominion and Territories as, not have been ceded to or purchased by Us, are reserved to them, or any of them, as their Hunting Grounds....

And We do further declare it to be Our Royal Will and Pleasure, for the present as aforesaid, to reserve under our Sovereignty, Protection, and Dominion, for the use of the said Indians, all the Lands and Territories not included within the Limits of Our said Three new Governments, or within the Limits of the Territory granted to the Hudson's Bay Company, as also all the Lands and Territories lying to the Westward of the Sources of Rivers which fall into the Sea from the West and Northwest as aforesaid.

And We do hereby strictly forbid, on Pain of our Displeasure, all our loving Subjects from making any Purchases or Settlements whatever, or taking Possession of any Lands above reserved, without our especial leave and Licence for that Purpose first obtained. And We do further strictly enjoin and require all Persons whatever who have either wilfully or inadvertently seated themselves upon any Lands within the Countries above described, or upon any other Lands which, not having been ceded to or purchased by Us, are still reserved to the said Indians as aforesaid, forthwith to remove themselves from such Settlements.

And whereas great Frauds and Abuses have been committed in purchasing Lands of the Indians, to the great Prejudice of our Interests, and to the great Dissatisfaction of the said Indians: In order, therefore to prevent such Irregularities for the future, and to the end that the Indians may be convinced of our Justice and determined Resolution to remove all reasonable Cause of Discontent, We do, with the Advice of our Privy Council strictly enjoin and require, that no private Person do presume to make any purchases from the said Indians, within those parts of our Colonies where, We have thought Proper to allow Settlement; but that, if at any Time any of the Said Indians should be inclined to dispose of the said Lands, the same shall be Purchased only for Us, in our Name, at some public Meeting or Assembly of the said Indians, to be held for the Purpose by the Governor or Commander in Chief of our Colony respectively within which they shall lie ....

Given at our Court at St. James the 7th Day of October 1763, in the Third Year of our Reign.

God Save the King

APOLOGY FOR RESIDENTIAL SCHOOLS

This is an excerpt of an apology by the Canadian Government, on behalf of Canadians, for the Indian Residential School System. It was read by Prime Minister Stephen Harper in Parliament on 11 June 2008.

APOLOGY ON BEHALF OF CANADIANS FOR THE INDIAN RESIDENTIAL SCHOOL SYSTEM

The treatment of children in Indian Residential Schools is a sad chapter in our history.

For more than a century, Indian Residential Schools separated over 150,000 Aboriginal children from their families and communities. In the 1870s, the federal government, partly in order to meet its obligation to educate Aboriginal children, began to play a role in the development and administration of these schools. Two primary objectives of the Residential Schools system were to remove and isolate children from the influence of their homes, families, traditions and cultures, and to assimilate them into the dominant culture. These objectives were based on the assumption Aboriginal cultures and spiritual beliefs were inferior and unequal. Indeed, some sought, as it was infamously said, "to kill the Indian in the child." Today, we recognize that this policy of assimilation was wrong, has caused great harm, and has no place in our country.

One hundred and thirty-two federally-supported schools were located in every province and territory, except Newfoundland, New Brunswick and Prince Edward Island. Most schools were operated as "joint ventures" with Anglican, Catholic, Presbyterian or United Churches. The Government of Canada built an educational system in which very young children were often forcibly removed from their homes, often taken far from their communities. Many were inadequately fed, clothed and housed. All were deprived of the care and nurturing of their parents, grandparents and communities. First Nations, Inuit and Métis languages and cultural practices were prohibited in these schools. Tragically, some of these children died while attending residential schools and others never returned home.

The government now recognizes that the consequences of the Indian Residential Schools policy were profoundly negative and that this policy has had a lasting and damaging impact on Aboriginal culture, heritage and language. While some former students have spoken positively about their experiences at residential schools, these stories are far overshadowed by tragic accounts of the emotional, physical and sexual abuse and neglect of helpless children, and their separation from powerless families and communities.

The legacy of Indian Residential Schools has contributed to social problems that continue to exist in many communities today.

It has taken extraordinary courage for the thousands of survivors that have come forward to speak publicly about the abuse they suffered. It is a testament to their resilience as individuals and to the strength of their cultures. Regrettably, many former students are not with us today and died never having received a full apology from the Government of Canada.

The government recognizes that the absence of an apology has been an impediment to healing and reconciliation. Therefore, on behalf of the Government of Canada and all Canadians, I stand before you, in this Chamber so central to our life as a country, to apologize to Aboriginal peoples for Canada's role in the Indian Residential Schools system.

To the approximately 80,000 living former students, and all family members and communities, the Government of Canada now recognizes that it was wrong to forcibly remove children from their homes and we apologize for having done this. We now recognize that it was wrong to separate children from rich and vibrant cultures and traditions that it created a void in many lives and communities, and we apologize for having done this. We now recognize that, in separating children from their families, we undermined the ability of many to adequately parent their own children and sowed the seeds for generations to follow, and we apologize for having done this. We now recognize that, far too often, these institutions gave rise to abuse or neglect and were inadequately controlled, and we apologize for failing to protect you. Not only did you suffer these abuses as children, but as you became parents, you were powerless to protect your own children from suffering the same experience, and for this we are sorry.

The burden of this experience has been on your shoulders for far too long. The burden is properly ours as a Government, and as a country. There is no place in Canada for the attitudes that inspired the Indian Residential Schools system to ever prevail again. You have been working on recovering from this experience for a long time and in a very real sense, we are now joining you on this journey. The Government of Canada sincerely apologizes and asks the forgiveness of the Aboriginal peoples of this country for failing them so profoundly.

Nous le regrettons
We are sorry
Nimitataynan
Niminchinowesamin
Mamiattugut

APOLOGY TO THE NATIVE PEOPLES OF THE UNITED STATES

This apology was contained within the Department of Defense Appropriation Act, 2010 (Public Law 111–118). It was enacted on 19 December 2009.

APOLOGY TO THE NATIVE PEOPLES OF THE UNITED STATES

Sec. 8113. (A) Acknowledgment and Apology.—The United States, acting through Congress—

(1) recognizes the special legal and political relationship Indian tribes have with the United States and the solemn covenant with the land we share;

(2) commends and honors Native Peoples for the thousands of years that they have stewarded and protected this land;

(3) recognizes that there have been years of official depredations, ill-conceived policies, and the breaking of covenants by the Federal Government regarding Indian tribes;

(4) apologizes on behalf of the people of the United States to all Native Peoples for the many instances of violence, maltreatment, and neglect inflicted on Native Peoples by citizens of the United States;

(5) expresses its regret for the ramifications of former wrongs and its commitment to build on the positive relationships of the past and present to move toward a brighter future where all the people of this land live reconciled as brothers and sisters, and harmoniously steward and protect this land together;

(6) Urges the President to acknowledge the wrongs of the United States against Indian tribes in the history of the United States in order to bring healing to this land; and

(7) Commends the State governments that have begun reconciliation efforts with recognized Indian tribes located in their boundaries and encourages all State governments similarly to work toward reconciling relationships with Indian tribes within their boundaries.

(b) DISCLAIMER.—Nothing in this section—

(1) authorizes or supports any claim against the United States; or

(2) serves as a settlement of claim against the United States.

STUDYING THE INDIGENOUS PEOPLES OF NORTH AMERICA

This appendix is for those wishing to delve deeper into some of the broad topics covered in this book. The focus is on anthropological studies.

ETHNOGRAPHIC FIELDWORK

Two things are fundamentally important for doing ethnographic field-work among Indigenous peoples of North America: permission of the people being studied, and formal training in ethnography. Ethnographic research on the Indigenous peoples of North America is usually best left to professional anthropologists, graduate students (i.e., those working on a master's degree or PhD), or undergraduates enrolled in an ethnographic field school. Before undertaking ethnographic research it is important to understand the complexities of ethnographic method, theory, ethics, and protocols, which are usually dependent on substantial amounts of previous coursework as well as direction from professional ethnographers and representatives of the Indigenous group one wishes to study. Taking photos of people, places, or events without permission, for example, may lead to serious consequences, and issues regarding intellectual property rights and ownership and the dissemination of information should all be dealt with and agreed upon before any kind of fieldwork begins.

The web page of the American Anthropological Association (AAA) is a good place to start for those considering cultural anthropology as a career (www.aaanet.org).

ARCHAEOLOGICAL FIELDWORK

Archaeology in North America is governed by law. In most cases it is illegal to disturb archaeological sites without a permit issued by the government, which usually requires a graduate degree and extensive field experience. Penalties include jail time as well as fines. Some jurisdictions also require consultation with local Indigenous groups before excavation, and some Indigenous groups have their own permit system for conducting archaeological investigations in their territory, independent of federal, state, or provincial permit systems.

Those wishing to become involved in prehistoric archaeology in North America are well advised to enroll in one of the many archaeology field schools offered by colleges and universities. Many archaeological projects have public education programs and some projects actively pursue volunteer participation. Information on these can often be found in local media, through local or regional archaeological associations or societies, or through local colleges and universities. The web page of the Society for American Archaeology (SAA) is a good place to start for those considering archaeology as a career (www.saa.org).

MAJOR PRINT AND WEB RESOURCES
For those seeking more information about the Indigenous peoples and cultures of North America through written and Internet sources, the following are some good places to start.

Handbook of North American Indians
The *Handbook of North American Indians* is a series of volumes, published by the Smithsonian Institution beginning in 1978 under the general editorship of William C. Sturtevant. Fifteen of the planned 20 volumes were published up until 2008 when the series was suspended. Each volume contains numerous articles by leading scholars in the field, with separate volume editors. The series has become a standard reference.

Published volumes include *Volume 2: Indians in Contemporary Society* (2008); *Volume 3: Environment, Origins, and Population* (2006); *Volume 4: History of Indian–White Relations* (1988); *Volume 5: Arctic* (1984); *Volume 6: Subarctic* (1981); *Volume 7: Northwest Coast* (1990); *Volume 8: California* (1990); *Volumes 9 and 10: Southwest* (1979 and 1983); *Volume 11: Great Basin* (1986); *Volume 12: Plateau* (1998); *Volume 13: Plains* (2001); *Volume 14: Southeast* (2004); *Volume 15: Northeast* (1978); and *Volume 17: Languages* (1997).

Journals
The major journals mentioned here either (i) focus on North American Indigenous peoples and cultures, or (ii) are international in scope, but occasionally include articles on North American Indigenous peoples and

cultures. They are major journals from the fields of anthropology and indigenous studies (or Native American Studies, American Indian Studies, etc.). Major journals from other disciplines that sometimes focus on the Indigenous peoples can be found in the fields of history, human geography, law, psychology, sociology, the fine and performing arts, and others, but are not included here. Researchers interested in a particular region should also consider the many fine regional journals focusing on the social sciences and humanities.

Major journals that focus particularly on Indigenous peoples and cultures of North America include *American Indian Culture and Research Journal*; *American Indian Quarterly*; the *Canadian Journal of Indigenous Studies*; *Native Studies Review*; and the *European Review of Native American Studies*.

Major anthropology journals that are international in scope but occasionally include articles on North American Indigenous groups or issues include *American Anthropologist, Current Anthropology, American Ethnologist, Ethnology*, and *Anthropologica*.

Major journals that focus specifically on North American archaeology include *American Antiquity, Canadian Journal of Archaeology, North American Archaeologist*, and *Historical Archaeology*. Other major archaeology journals that occasionally include articles on North American archaeology include *Journal of Anthropological Archaeology, Journal of Archaeological Method and Theory, Journal of Archaeological Research, Journal of Archaeological Science, Journal of Field Archaeology*, and *World Archaeology*.

AlterNatives: An International Journal of Indigenous Peoples includes articles about the Indigenous peoples of North America.

Book Publishers

Scholarly books on Indigenous peoples are mostly published through university presses. Prominent university presses well-known for their Indigenous peoples and cultures publishing programs include Cambridge University Press, Oxford University Press, University of Arizona Press, University of British Columbia Press, University of California Press, University of Kansas Press, University of Nebraska Press, University of New Mexico Press, University of North Carolina Press, University of Oklahoma Press, University of Toronto Press, University of Washington Press, and Yale University Press. Researchers are encouraged to peruse the catalogs of university presses in their geographic area of interest.

Although it is mostly university presses that publish scholarly anthropology books, there are some commercial publishers that publish on the topic as well. Left Coast Press is one such press. Some Indigenous nations have also begun their own book publishing programs, creating some very good results.

Human Relations Area Files (HRAF)

The Human Relations Area Files are comprised of the text of ethnographies and archaeological reports from around the world. They are useful for undertaking cross-cultural comparisons. Access is by subscription. Many libraries are subscribed.

National Indigenous Organizations

Canada: Assembly of First Nations (www.afn.ca)
United States: National Congress of American Indians (www.ncai.org)

Federal Government Agencies

United States: Bureau of Indian Affairs (www.bia.gov)
Canada: Aboriginal Affairs and Northern Development Canada (www.aandc-aadnc.gc.ca)

International Indigenous Studies

United Nations Permanent Forum on Indigenous Issues (www.un.org/esa/socdev/unpfii)

Indigenous Groups

Many Indigenous groups have their own websites. Many of these can be easily found through an Internet search for the group or through links from a national Indigenous organization or a government agency.

Multimedia News and Information

There are many Native-operated news and information organizations, often serving regional or local audiences and readerships. The largest and best-known national multi-media organization is Indian Country Today, which publishes the weekly newspaper *Indian Country Today,* has podcasts, and disseminates information through its website (www.indiancountrytoday medianetwork.com).

Isuma.tv (www.isuma.tv) is an Inuit-run network of Indigenous media focusing on providing access to online Indigenous channels and films. It allows Indigenous peoples from around the globe to upload and exchange multimedia content, but the focus is on North American groups.

The Smithsonian Institution

The Anthropology Outreach Office at the Smithsonian Institution (http://anthropology.si.edu/outreach/outrch1.html) provides links to many resources on North American Indigenous groups, both on the Internet and in print, including a critical bibliography of more than 800 books.

Film

Reel Injun is a 2009 documentary by Cree filmmaker Neil Diamond exploring the depictions of Native Americans through the history of Hollywood filmmaking. (Available on DVD.)

Indian Country Diaries is a documentary film series originally appearing on PBS in 2006. (Available on DVD.)

GLOSSARY

Aboriginal On a global scale, Aboriginal is synonymous with Indigenous. In Canada, Aboriginal is a legal term encompassing the Indians, Inuit, and Metis.

Acculturation Culture change resulting when two or more cultures come in contact, sometimes based on direct or indirect force from a dominant culture. The term is usually used in reference to the changes brought about by a dominant culture on another culture.

Adobe A material used in the manufacture of traditional houses among Indigenous peoples of the Southwest culture area. Contains a mixture of clay, water, organic material, and sometimes sand.

Agriculture Full-scale farming, including animals being used to plow fields. Usually also includes large-scale irrigation and the use of fertilizers.

Alaska Natives The Indigenous peoples of Alaska, including Indians, Aleutians, and Eskimos.

Animism The belief that, besides humans, many other animate and inanimate objects contain spirits.

Anthropology The study of humans from evolutionary, comparative, and holistic perspectives.

Archaeological Site A location where there is physical evidence of past human activity.

Archaeology The study of humans through the physical remains of their activities. In North America, archaeology is usually considered a branch of anthropology.

Art The enhancement of material culture or performance for aesthetic purposes. For example, utilitarian objects or houses may be enhanced by paintings. Rituals may be enhanced by dancing or dramatic storytelling.

Artifact Any portable object that shows physical evidence of being made or used by people.

Assimilation Culture change resulting from the adoption of traits from a different culture.

Atlatl Spear thrower.

Band In a broad anthropological context, a band is usually a group of less than 50 people with loose ties based on kinship acting as an independent political unit, and is most characteristic of generalized foragers. In Canada, band continues to be used as a legal term to describe "a body of Indians for which money has been set aside." In this second context, band is now synonymous with nation or First Nation.

Beringia A large, unglaciated area of land connecting North America to Asia during the last ice age.

Biological Anthropology The branch of anthropology that focuses on human biology, including skeletal remains and genetics.

Blood Quantum The proportion of Indian blood that a person has. Blood quantum is used by many groups and the US government to establish whether they qualify for membership or benefits.

Carrying Capacity The maximum number of people that can be supported by the resources in a specified area.

CDIB Abbreviation for "Certificate of Degree of Indian Blood," issued by the United States Bureau of Indian Affairs to specify the percentage of Indian blood a person has.

Chief In a broad anthropological context, a chief is the leader of a chiefdom. In contemporary Indigenous societies in North America, Chief often designates an elected and/or hereditary leader of an Indigenous group.

Chiefdom A form of political organization with a recognized leader, based on heredity, who is the authority for a substantially large population spread out through multiple communities. Usually associated with horticultural groups.

Cigar Store Indian A carving of an Indigenous person, usually depicted in traditional regalia from the Plains culture area. Historically, they were placed on the sidewalk in front of a tobacco shop. Today, they continue to be used for advertising and decoration in many contexts beyond tobacco.

Clan A unilineal descent group in which all members believe they have common ancestry, although some of the links are unknown.

Clovis Technologically, Clovis is a particular style of fluted projectile point associated with the hunting of megafauna during the Paleo-Indian period. They date to about 12,000–11,000 years ago and are usually several centimeters long. Clovis also refers to the culture and people associated with the projectile point (i.e., Clovis culture; Clovis people).

Colonialism The process of a European nation occupying a land already occupied by Indigenous people and then subjugating and dominating them.

Coprolites Preserved feces; excrement.

Coyote A prominent character in the mythology of many Indigenous groups. Usually a trickster and sometimes a transformer.

CRM An abbreviation for cultural resource management.

Cultural Anthropology The branch of anthropology that focuses on the cultures of contemporary people and those of the recent past. Ethnography and ethnology are associated with cultural anthropology.

Cultural Relativism The notion that a culture should not be judged using the standards of another.

Cultural Resource Management Archaeology being done in advance of development projects that could potentially impact archaeological sites.

Culture The shared and learned things that people have (material culture), think (ideology), and do (customs).

Culture Area A large geographical area in which many different societies share similar cultural traits. A heuristic device for studying the Indigenous peoples of North America in prehistoric and historic times.

Culture Hero A character in myths that is responsible for creating many of the important parts of nature and culture.

Culture History A description of the sequence of events in an area, usually referring to prehistory. The focus is on description rather than explanation.

Descent Group A grouping of individuals dependent on biological relationships, including lineages and clans.

Diffusion The spread of ideas.

Ecofacts Plant and animal remains from archaeological sites.

Egalitarian A form of social and political organization where everybody has roughly equal status.

Emic An insider's perspective, such as an Indigenous person's description or analysis based on concepts that are meaningful in her or his own culture.

Enrolled In the United States, having membership in a tribal entity.

Eskimo Indigenous peoples of the Arctic. The term has been largely replaced with "Inuit" in Canada and Greenland.

Ethnographic Analogy Using ethnographies to make inferences about the past. This is often used by archaeologists in interpreting archaeological remains. If, for example, an ethnographer indicated that a certain size and style of house typically housed 30 people, and an archaeologist discovered a similar size and style of house from an earlier time in the same region, she or he would use ethnographic analogy to suggest that this house probably housed about 30 people as well.

Ethnographic Present Describing pre-European lifeways as if people were still practicing them the same way. This was characteristic of ethnographies written in the late 1800s and early 1900s.

Ethnography A written description of a culture based on first-hand observation.

Etic An outsider's perspective, such as that of an anthropologist's description or analysis using concepts meaningful to other anthropologists, rather than those of the people being studied.

Eurocentrism Focused on Europe, especially the view that European cultures are superior to cultures elsewhere.

Exploitation Colonialism A form of colonialism with the primary goal of extracting existing resources, and involving few colonists.

Extended Family A nuclear family and associated kin from the same or other generations.

Fire Hearths The location of controlled fires within archaeological sites, indicated by accumulations of charred wood and ash.

First Nations Common terminology for describing those formerly known as Indians in Canada. It also often replaces the legal term of "Indian band" in Canada.

First Peoples Often used as a replacement for the term "Indians" in Canada.

Fluted Point A projectile point that has a longitudinal channel removed from the base. Clovis points are one kind of fluted point.

Fluted Point Tradition A unique way of making projectile points by removing a channel at the base of the point. The function of the channel is not known, but most believe that it was to facilitate quick hafting to a spear or to accommodate blood loss from a speared animal. Fluted points are usually associated with the hunting of mega fauna during the Paleo-Indian period.

Folsom A variant of the fluted point tradition.

Foragers People whose diet is dependent on wild plants and animals. Also known as hunters and gatherers.

Frontier Theory A framework used in some recent ethnographies, in which the culture of recent and contemporary First Nations is considered in the context of Euro-American assumptions that the land and resources were free for the taking; that Euro-Americans were superior; that Indigenous peoples were incapable of proper resource management; and that Indigenous peoples were an impediment to progress.

Generalized Foraging Depending on a wide diversity of wild plants and animals.

Historical Particularism Understanding each culture as a product of its own evolution.

Hogan A kind of house common in the Southwest, usually associated with the Navajo.

Holism Understanding that all parts of a culture are interrelated.

Horticulture Farming with hand tools.

House A basic unit of economic and social organization among Indigenous groups of the Northwest Coast. Members of a house lived in large, communal, cedar plank houses during winter months.

Ideology The worldview, belief systems, and values of a group.

Igloo A house made of snow blocks, associated with the Inuit.

Indian In North America, "Indian" is used in a narrow, legal sense to define a particular type of Indigenous person. As well, in a broader sense, it is often used synonymously with Native or Aboriginal.

Indian Lands Used to describe lands—both in the United States and Canada—that have been set aside for use by Indigenous peoples, including but not restricted to reserves and reservations.

Indigenous In North America, an umbrella term to capture all the peoples and groups that claim ancestry to the people who occupied the lands before the arrival of Europeans. Globally, the term is often applied to minority populations that have been in the area for very long periods and who have been dominated economically, socially, and politically by others.

Indios Those who speak an Indigenous language in Mexico.

Inuit The Indigenous peoples of the Arctic in Canada and Greenland, formerly known as Eskimos in those regions.

Inuksuk A stone structure created by Inuit; traditionally used as markers, hunting and navigation aids, and message centers. Some were in the form of humans.

Kinship Relationships determined through blood or marriage.

Kinship Group A social group based on relatedness through blood or marriage.

Lineage A descent group in which all the linkages between members are known.

Linguistics The study of languages.

Longhouse A multi-family house typical of traditional Northeast culture, constructed of saplings, poles, and bark.

Maritime Adaptation An adaptation to resources from the ocean.

Matrilineal Tracing descent through the female line.

Mesoamerica Roughly equivalent to Middle America, or Central America; the lands between the Panama Canal and a line running east–west through northern Mexico. This is the area that was dominated by the Mayan and Aztec empires in earlier times.

Mestizo Those of mixed ancestry in Mexico.

Metis One of the three federally recognized categories of Aboriginal people in Canada; descendants of mixed Indigenous/European ancestry, mostly from encounters with French fur traders in the colonial period.

Middens A discrete accumulation of trash; a common type of archaeological site.

Myth A story involving the actions of supernatural characters in the past. In anthropology, the term does not imply that the story is false.

Mythology The study of myths.

NAGPRA The Native American Graves Protection and Repatriation Act, enacted by the United States in 1990. The act calls for the return of human skeletal remains and associated artifacts collected before 1990 to their associated Native groups, as well as for consultation with Native Americans when human remains are found or are expected to be found.

Native American Common terminology to describe the Indigenous peoples of the United States, including Indians and Alaska Natives.

Non-Status Indian In Canada, someone with Indigenous ancestry who is not registered with the federal government.

North America According to most anthropologists focusing on Indigenous peoples, the lands north of Mesoamerica and the Caribbean, including the northern part of Mexico, the continental United States, Canada, and Greenland.

Nuclear Family A family unit consisting of a mother, father, and offspring.

Nunavut A large area of land in northern Canada that is controlled by Inuit, with powers roughly equivalent to a province or state.

Outaluck In the United States, an unofficial term applied to those who would like to be enrolled, but aren't.

Participant-Observation A method used by anthropologists doing ethnographic research, in which she or he is an active participant in the community as well as an observer.

Pastoralism Subsistence based on the herding of domestic animals. Prior to the arrival of Europeans, no North American Indigenous groups were pastoralists.

Patrilineal Descent traced through the male line.

Pemmican A form of dried meat commonly used in the Subarctic and Plains culture areas.

Petroglyph One of the major kinds of rock art; carving or pecking into boulders or rock outcrops.

Peyote A cactus that produces a narcotic effect.

Pictograph A major kind of rock art; painting on rock outcrops.

Pithouse A semi-subterranean dwelling, typically constructed with a pole framework and covered with earth.

Politics of Embarrassment A strategy used by Indigenous groups that involves bringing wrongdoings of governments against Indigenous peoples to light on national and international stages. This is done in the hopes that the governments will then change their practices and policies to avoid further embarrassment.

Pothunters People who loot archaeological sites. The name is derived from people who are looking for pottery, but is now applied as a generic term for looters of archaeological sites.

Potlatch A ceremony common among Northwest Coast groups that involves feasting, recitations of oral history, and gift-giving. The explicit function of potlatches is to confirm an event of social significance, but they also serve many other social, political, and ideological purposes.

Potsherd A broken piece of pottery.

Powwow A ceremony or event involving dancing and singing that brings together different groups. Traditionally, it was likely restricted largely to the Plains, but it is now widespread.

Prehistory The time period before written forms of language existed in an area. In North America, the transition between prehistory and history occurred when Europeans arrived in each area.

Projectile Points Arrowheads, spear points, and atlatl darts.

Radiocarbon Dating Determining how old organic remains are by determining how much carbon 14 is left in them.

Raven A prominent character in myths, particularly those of the Northwest Coast.

Recall Ethnography A description of lifeways based on the memories of individuals from their own experiences, or those recalling how earlier times were described to them.

Registered Indian In Canada, someone who is on a list maintained by the federal government.

Reservation Land set aside by the government for use by specific Indigenous groups of the United States.

Reserve Lands set aside by the government for use by specific Indigenous groups of Canada.

Salvage Ethnography Doing ethnography with the idea that the information is being collected before its imminent loss.

Settler Colonialism A type of colonialism that depends on colonists from the colonizing nation to settle in substantial numbers and then create new resources, such as by farming.

Shaman A religious specialist in Indigenous groups who has a special relationship with the supernatural world.

Shell Midden A discrete accumulation of trash with a visible component of shell. Very common kind of archaeological site in coastal areas.

Sodality Also known as pan-tribal association. A common-interest association that includes members from various settlements in tribes.

Specialized Foraging A subsistence strategy depending on wild plants and animals but specializing in one particular resource, such as salmon on the Northwest Coast and acorns in California. Also known as complex foraging.

Status Card In Canada, a card issued by the federal government identifying the person as a registered Indian.

Status Indian In Canada, another name for a registered Indian—someone who is federally recognized as an Indian.

Stratified When a society is divided into various classes, such as high, middle, and lower classes.

Time Immemorial Words sometimes used by Indigenous people, roughly translating as "forever."

Tipi (or Teepee) A type of shelter typically used by Plains groups; involves animal skins laid over a conical pole frame.

Tipi Ring The circle of stones that originally weighed down the edges of the hide portion of a tipi. When people moved camp they would take the tipis, but leave the stones as they were.

Traditional Lifeways In North American anthropology, this usually refers to the culture of Indigenous groups as they were immediately before the arrival of Europeans, aspects of which may continue to present times.

Transformer Prominent characters in myths of Indigenous peoples who could transform animate and inanimate objects into whatever they wished.

Tribal Entity In the United States, an Indian tribe or Alaska Native village.

Tribe A form of political organization in which groups of people are typically led by a bigman or headman, which is often an informal position. Communities are tied together through kinship and sodalities.

Trickster Prominent characters in myths of Indigenous peoples who often did good as a byproduct of deceit, mischief, and trickery. Prominent tricksters include Coyote and Raven.

Turtle Island An alternate name for North America, used by some Indigenous peoples.

Vision quest A common ritual among many Indigenous groups in which an individual goes on a solitary quest seeking a guardian spirit that appears in a vision.

Wannabee In the United States, an unofficial term sometimes used to describe those who want to be recognized as an Indian by the federal government or by their tribal group, but who do not meet the requirements.

BIBLIOGRAPHY

Adams, David Wallace. 1995. *Education for Extinction: American Indians and the Boarding School Experience, 1875–1928.* Lawrence, KS: University Press of Kansas.

Alfred, Taiaiake. 2009. *Peace, Power, Righteousness: An Indigenous Manifesto.* 2nd ed. New York: Oxford University Press.

Bailey, Garrick A., ed. 2008. *Handbook of North American Indians.* Vol. 2. *Indians in Contemporary Society.* Washington, DC: Smithsonian Institution.

Basso, Keith H. 1996. *Wisdom Sits in Places: Landscape and Language among the Western Apache.* Albuquerque, NM: University of New Mexico Press.

Bastian, Dawn E., and Judy K. Mitchell. 2004. *Handbook of Native American Mythology.* New York: Oxford University Press.

Belanger, Yale D. 2010. *Ways of Knowing: An Introduction to Native Studies in Canada.* Toronto, ON: Nelson.

Berkhofer, Robert F., Jr. 1978. *The White Man's Indian: Images of the American Indian from Columbus to the Present.* New York: Vintage Books.

Berlo, Janet C., and Ruth B. Phillips. 1998. *Native North American Art.* New York: Oxford University Press.

Berman, Tressa. 2008. "Cultural Appropriation." In *A Companion to the Anthropology of American Indians*, ed. Thomas Biolsi, 383–97. Malden, MA: Blackwell.

Biolsi, Thomas, ed. 2008. *A Companion to the Anthropology of American Indians.* Malden, MA: Blackwell.

Biolsi, Thomas, and Larry J. Zimmerman, eds. 1997. *Indians and Anthropologists: Vine Deloria Jr., and the Critique of Anthropology.* Tucson, AZ: University of Arizona Press.

Bird, S. Elizabeth, ed. 1996. *Dressing in Feathers: The Construction of the Indian in American Popular Culture.* Boulder, CO: Westview Press.

Bohannan, Paul, and Mark Glazer, eds. 1988. *High Points in Anthropology.* 2nd ed. New York: Knopf.

Brescia, Michael M., and John C. Super. 2009. *North America: An Introduction.* Toronto, ON: University of Toronto Press.

Brock, Kathy. 2008. "Rhetoric, Reality, and Rights: Comparing Canadian and American Aboriginal Policy." In *Canada and the United States: Differences that Count.* 3rd ed., ed. David M. Thomas and Barbara Boyle Torrey, 271–90. Toronto, ON: University of Toronto Press.

Brody, Hugh. 2004. *Maps and Dreams: Indians and the British Columbia Frontier.* Vancouver, BC: Douglas and McIntyre.

Brown, Michael F. 2004. *Who Owns Native Culture?* Cambridge, MA: Harvard University Press.

Bruchac, Margaret M., Siobahn M. Hart, and H. Martin Wobst, eds. 2010. *Indigenous Archaeologies: A Reader on Decolonization.* Walnut Creek, CA: Left Coast Press.

Buscombe, Edward. 2006. *Injun! Native Americans in the Movies.* London: Reaktion Books.

Cardinal, Harold. 1999. *The Unjust Society.* Vancouver, BC: Douglas and McIntyre. First published 1969.

Carino, Joji, Duane Champagne, Neva Collins, Myrna Cunningham, Daled Sambo Dorough, Naomi Kipuri, and Mililani Trask. 2009. *The State of the World's Indigenous Peoples.* New York: United Nations.

Cattelino, Jessica R. 2008. "Gaming." In *Handbook of North American Indians.* Vol. 2. *Indians in Contemporary Society,* ed. Garrick A. Bailey, 148–56. Washington, DC: Smithsonian Institution.

Cattelino, Jessica R. 2010. "Anthropologies of the United States." *Annual Review of Anthropology* 39 (1): 275–92. http://dx.doi.org/10.1146/annurev.anthro.012809.104927.

Cote, Charlotte. 2010. *Spirits of Our Whaling Ancestors: Revitalizing Makah and Nuu-chah-nulth Traditions.* Seattle, WA: University of Washington Press.

Deloria, Ella. 1998. *Speaking of Indians.* Lincoln, NE: University of Nebraska Press. First published 1944.

Deloria, Philip J. 1998. *Playing Indian.* New Haven, CT: Yale University Press.

Deloria, Vine, Jr. 1988. *Custer Died for Your Sins: An Indian Manifesto.* Norman, OK: University of Oklahoma Press. First published 1969.

Deloria, Vine, Jr. 2003. *God is Red: A Native View of Religion.* 3rd ed. Golden, CO: Fulcrum.

Dickason, Olive Patricia, and David T. McNab. 2009. *Canada's First Nations: A History of Founding Peoples from Earliest Times.* 4th ed. Don Mills, ON: Oxford University Press Canada.

Fagan, Brian M. 2005. *Ancient North America: The Archaeology of a Continent*. 4th ed. New York: Thames and Hudson.

Francis, Daniel. 1992. *The Imaginary Indian: The Image of the Indian in Canadian Culture*. Vancouver, BC: Arsenal Pulp Press.

Garroutte, Eva Marie. 2003. *Real Indians: Identity and the Survival of Native America*. Berkeley, CA: University of California Press.

Garoutte, Eva Marie. 2008. "Native American Identity in Law." In *Handbook of North American Indians*. Vol. 2. *Indians in Contemporary Society,* ed. Garrick A. Bailey, 302–7. Washington, DC: Smithsonian Institution.

Goddard, Ives. 1996. "Introduction." In *Handbook of North American Indians*. Vol. 2. *Languages,* ed. Ives Goddard, 1–16. Washington, DC: Smithsonian Institution.

Goddard, Ives, ed. 1996. *Handbook of North American Indians*. Vol. 17. *Languages*. Washington, DC: Smithsonian Institution.

Harvard Project on American Indian Economic Development. 2008. *The State of Native Nations: Conditions under US Policies of Self-Determination*. New York: Oxford University Press.

Hedican, Edward J. 2008. *Applied Anthropology in Canada: Understanding Aboriginal Issues*. 2nd ed. Toronto, ON: University of Toronto Press.

Hill, Gord. 2009. *500 Years of Indigenous Resistance*. Oakland, CA: PM Press.

Jacknis, Ira. 2008. "'The Last Wild Indian in North America': Changing Museum Representations of Ishi." In *Museums and Difference*, ed. Daniel J. Sherman, 60–96. Indianapolis, IA: Indiana University Press.

Johnson, Daniel Morley. 2011. "From the Tomahawk Chop to the Road Block: Discourses of Savagism in Whitestream Media." *American Indian Quarterly* 35 (1): 104–34. http://dx.doi.org/10.5250/0095182X.35.1.104.

Kan, Sergei, ed. 2001. *Strangers to Relatives: The Adoption and Naming of Anthropologists in Native North America*. Lincoln, NE: University of Nebraska Press.

Kehoe, Alice Beck. 1998. *The Land of Prehistory: A Critical History of American Archaeology*. New York: Routledge.

Kehoe, Alice Beck. 2006. *North American Indians: A Comprehensive Account*. 3rd ed. Upper Saddle River, NJ: Pearson.

Kilpatrick, Jacquelin. 1999. *Celluloid Indians: Native Americans in Film*. Lincoln, NE: University of Nebraska Press.

King, C. Richard, ed. 2010. *The Native American Mascot Controversy: A Handbook*. Lanham, MD: Scarecrow Press.

Kroeber, Theodora. 1961. *Ishi in Two Worlds: A Biography of the Last Wild Indian in North America*. Berkeley, CA: University of California Press.

Lurie, Nancy O. 1988. "Relations between Indians and Anthropologists." In *Handbook of North American Indians*. Vol. 4. *History of Indian-White Relations,* ed. Wilcombe E. Washburn, 548–56. Washington, DC: Smithsonian Institution.

Maaka, Roger C.A., and Chris Andersen, eds. 2006. *The Indigenous Experience: Global Perspectives*. Toronto, ON: Canadian Scholars' Press.

McIlwraith, Thomas F. 2012. *"We Are Still Didene": Stories of Hunting and History from Northern British Columbia*. Toronto, ON: University of Toronto Press.

McMillan, Alan D., and Eldon Yellowhorn. 2004. *First Peoples of Canada*. Vancouver, BC: Douglas and McIntyre.

McNickle, D'Arcy. 1973. *Native American Tribalism: Indian Survivals and Renewals*. New York: Oxford University Press.

Medicine, Beatrice. 2001. *Learning to Be an Anthropologist and Remaining "Native": Selected Writings*. Chicago, IL: University of Illinois Press.

Meltzer, David J. 2009. *First Peoples in a New World: Colonizing Ice Age America*. Berkeley, CA: University of California Press.

Menzies, Charles R., ed. 2006. *Traditional Ecological Knowledge and Natural Resource Management*. Lincoln, NE: University of Nebraska Press.

Menzies, Charles R., and Caroline Butler. 2006. "Understanding Ecological Knowledge." In *Traditional Ecological Knowledge and Natural Resource Management*, ed. Charles R. Menzies, 1–17. Lincoln, NE: University of Nebraska Press.

Miller, J.R. 1996. *Shingwauk's Vision: A History of Native Residential Schools*. Toronto, ON: University of Toronto Press.

Milner, George R., and George Chaplin. 2010. "Eastern North American Population at ca. A.D. 1500." *American Antiquity* 75 (4): 707–26.

Moerman, Daniel E. 1998. *Native American Ethnobotany*. Portland, OR: Timber Press.

Moerman, Daniel E. 2009. *Native American Medicinal Plants: An Ethnobotanical Dictionary*. Portland, OR: Timber Press.

Moerman, Daniel E. 2010. *Native American Food Plants: An Ethnobotanical Dictionary*. Portland, OR: Timber Press.

Muckle, Robert J. 2006. *Introducing Archaeology*. Toronto, ON: University of Toronto Press.

Muckle, Robert J. 2007. *The First Nations of British Columbia: An Anthropological Survey*. 2nd ed. Vancouver, BC: University of British Columbia Press.

Muckle, Robert J., ed. 2008. *Reading Archaeology: An Introduction*. Toronto, ON: University of Toronto Press.

Nabokov, Peter, ed. 1999. *Native American Testimony, Revised Edition: A Chronicle of Indian-White Relations from Prophecy to the Present, 1492–2000*. New York: Penguin.

Neusius, Sarah W., and G. Timothy Gross. 2007. *Seeking Our Past: An Introduction to North American Archaeology*. New York: Oxford University Press.

Nichols, Roger L. 1998. *Indians in the United States and Canada: A Comparative History*. Lincoln, NE: University of Nebraska Press.

Niezen, Ronald. 2003. *The Origins of Indigenism: Human Rights and the Politics of Identity.* Berkeley, CA: University of California Press.

Niezen, Ronald. 2008. "The Global Indigenous Movement." In *Handbook of North American Indians.* Vol. 2. *Indians in Contemporary Society,* ed. Garrick A. Bailey, 438–45. Washington, DC: Smithsonian Institution.

Porter, Robert B. 2005. "The Demise of the Ongwehoweh and the Rise of the Native Americans: Redressing the Genocidal Act of Forcing American Citizenship upon Indigenous Peoples." In *Sovereignty, Colonialism, and the Indigenous Nations: A Reader,* ed. Robert Odawi Porter, 429–32. Durham, NC: Carolina Academic Press. First published 1999.

Porter, Robert Odawi, ed. 2005. *Sovereignty, Colonialism and the Indigenous Nations: A Reader.* Durham, NC: Carolina Academic Press.

Radin, Paul. [1956] 1969. *The Trickster: A Study in American Indian Mythology.* New York: Greenwood Press.

Rollins, Peter C., and John C. O'Conner, eds. 1998. *Hollywood's Indian: the Portrayal of Native Americans in Film.* Lexington, KY: University Press of Kentucky.

Royal Commission on Aboriginal Peoples. 1996. Report of the Royal Commission on Aboriginal Peoples. Ottawa, ON: Government of Canada. Accessed 13 March 2011. www.ainc-inac.gc.ca/ap/rrc-eng.asp.

Scheiber, Laura L., and Mark D. Mitchell, eds. 2010. *Across a Great Divide: Continuity and Change in Native North American Societies, 1400–1900.* Tucson, AZ: University of Arizona Press.

Simpson, Audra. 2011. "Settlement's Secret." *Cultural Anthropology* 26 (2): 205–17. http://dx.doi.org/10.1111/j.1548-1360.2011.01095.x.

Sissons, Jeffrey. 2005. *First Peoples: Indigenous Cultures and Their Futures.* London: Reaktion Books.

Smith, Andrea. 2009. *Indigenous Peoples and Boarding Schools: A Comparative Study.* New York: United Nations.

Smith, Paul Chaat. 2009. *Everything You Know about Indians is Wrong.* Minneapolis, MN: University of Minnesota Press.

Snow, Dean R. 2010. *Archaeology of Native North America.* Upper Saddle River, NJ: Prentice Hall.

Starn, Orin. 2011. "Here Come the Anthros (Again): The Strange Marriage of Anthropology and Native America." *Cultural Anthropology* 26 (2): 179–204. http://dx.doi.org/10.1111/j.1548-1360.2011.01094.x.

Steckley, John L. 2008. *White Lies about the Inuit.* Toronto, ON: University of Toronto Press.

Stern, Pamela, and Lisa Stevenson. 2006. *Critical Inuit Studies: An Anthology of Contemporary Arctic Ethnography.* Lincoln, NE: University of Nebraska Press.

Strong, Pauline Turner. 2005. "Recent Ethnographic Research on North American Indigenous Peoples." *Annual Review of Anthropology* 34 (1): 253–68. http://dx.doi.org/10.1146/annurev.anthro.34.081804.120446.

Sturm, Circe. 2002. *Blood Politics: Race, Culture, and Identity in the Cherokee Nation of Oklahoma*. Berkeley, CA: University of California Press.

Sturtevant, William C. ed. 1978–2008. *Handbook of North American Indians*. Washington, DC: Smithsonian Institution.

Sutton, Mark Q. 2008. *An Introduction to Native North America*. 3rd ed. New York: Pearson.

Sutton, Mark Q. 2011. *A Prehistory of North America*. Upper Saddle River, NJ: Prentice-Hall.

Thornton, Russell. 2008. "Historical Demography." In *A Companion to the Anthropology of American Indians*, ed. Thomas Biolsi, 24–35. Malden, MA: Blackwell.

Trigger, Bruce G., and Wilcombe E. Washburn, eds. 1996. *North America*. The Cambridge History of the Native Peoples of the Americas, vol. 1. Cambridge: Cambridge University Press.

Ubelaker, Douglas H. 2006. "Population Size, Contact to Nadir." In *Handbook of North American Indians*. Vol. 3. *Environment, Origins, and Population*, ed. Douglas H. Ubelaker, 694–701. Washington, DC: Smithsonian Institution.

Ubelaker, Douglas H., ed. 2006. *Handbook of North American Indians*. Vol. 3. *Environment, Origins, and Population*. Washington, DC: Smithsonian Institution.

Walker, Renee B, and Boyce N. Driskell, eds. 2007. *Foragers of the Terminal Pleistocene in North America*. Lincoln, NE: University of Nebraska Press.

Warry, Wayne. 2008. *Ending Denial: Understanding Aboriginal Issues*. Toronto, ON: University of Toronto Press.

Washburn, Wilcomb E., ed. 1988. *Handbook of North American Indians*. Vol. 4. *History of Indian–White Relations*. Washington, DC: Smithsonian Institution.

Watkins, Joe. 2005. "Through Wary Eyes: Indigenous Perspectives on Archaeology." *Annual Review of Anthropology* 34 (1): 429–49. http://dx.doi.org/10.1146/annurev.anthro.34.081804.120540.

Webster, Gloria Cranmer. 1992. "From Colonization to Repatriation." In *Indigena: Contemporary Native Perspectives*, ed. Gerald McMaster and Lee-Ann Martin, 25–37. Vancouver, BC: Douglas and McIntyre.

Weston, Mary Ann. 1996. *Native Americans in the News: Images of Indians in the Twentieth Century Press*. Westport, CT: Greenwood Press.

INDEX

California
Sub-arctic
Plateau
great Basin

Use Infohawk